Careers for You Series

McGraw-Hill's

CAREERS FOR

FASHION PLATES

& Other Trendsetters

LUCIA MAURO

THIRD EDITION

New York Chicago San Francisco Lisbon London Madrid Mexico City
Milan New Delhi San Juan Seoul Singapore Sydney Toronto

The *McGraw·Hill* Companies

Library of Congress Cataloging-in-Publication Data

Mauro, Lucia.
      Careers for fashion plates & other trendsetters / by Lucia Mauro — 3rd ed.
         p.   cm. — (McGraw-Hill careers for you series)
         ISBN 0-07-149318-2 (alk. paper)
         1. Fashion—Vocational guidance. 2. Fashion design—Vocational guidance.
      3. Fashion merchandising—Vocational guidance. 4. Clothing trade—Vocational
guidance. I. Title.

TT507.M3787 2008
746.9′2023—dc22   2007047023

1 2 3 4 5 6 7 8 9 10 11 12 13 14 15 16 17 18 19   DOC/DOC   0 9 8

ISBN 978-0-07-149318-5
MHID   0-07-149318-2

McGraw-Hill books are available at special quantity discounts to use as premiums and sales promotions or for use in corporate training programs. To contact a representative, please visit the Contact Us pages at www.mhprofessional.com.

This book is printed on acid-free paper.

McGraw-Hill's

CAREERS FOR

FASHION PLATES

& Other Trendsetters

To Joe

Contents

Foreword

I am honored to write the foreword for Lucia Mauro's third edition of *Careers for Fashion Plates & Other Trendsetters*. This is an up-to-date account of real life in the fashion world, with a message to be flexible and keep an open mind to the increasingly important role of technology in the workplace.

Fashion is one of the most dynamic fields in the world, and with six seasonal changes per year, you are assured a creative life! The beauty, as I have found in the fashion field, is that one can try different careers under the fashion umbrella. Maintaining flexibility increases the chance of a more lucrative career on any career path. You will find that, at certain times in your life, different energy levels are required as you adjust to the demands of your personal life. For instance, I owned a custom suit shop until I discovered I was pregnant with twins. I was able to move into a fashion editor's position at a local publication, which allowed me to write on my own time. My store, on the other hand, required that I be present and ready to serve six days a week. Fashion is a flexible career.

It's also an industry of constant changes. Technology is a new force in the marketplace. To remain competitive, I recommend that as students you explore the possibilities and applications of software programs and the Internet. You will discover easy access to the world of fashion from your computer.

Being a fashion plate is good, steady work and a career you will enjoy for a lifetime.

Maureen Costello
Image Management Expert
Former Style Director with Paul Stuart, Chicago

CHAPTER ONE

Designing Your Fashion Career

What people wear is often a good indicator of their personality. Clothing, jewelry, shoes—they're fun and accessible ways to express oneself. Legends, such as Audrey Hepburn, Jacqueline Kennedy, and Princess Diana, and more recent tabloid stars—from Lindsay Lohan to Paris Hilton—are most closely identified with their couture. They've actually driven fashion trends. Together with its love of celebrity, our style-conscious society can admit to an obsession with clothing and accessories. Some of the largest floors of department stores are those that sell garments and their accoutrements. Mail-order and online catalogs feature an abundance of merchandise, from blue jeans to earrings to snow boots and cocktail suits.

Movies, such as *The Devil Wears Prada* (starring Meryl Streep as a dragon lady fashion editor) and Bravo TV's cult series "Project Runway," present an inside view of the multibillion-dollar fashion industry—its eccentricity, creativity, and influence worldwide. And, as long as we don't revert to our birthday suits, fashion will remain a lucrative career choice.

Just because clothing is in such great demand, however, doesn't guarantee everyone entry into this intense, often viciously competitive arena. Across the board, whether you pursue design, sales, retail, modeling, fashion photography, or public relations, the high-fashion universe is all-encompassing, demanding, and relentlessly fast paced, with heavy reliance on networking and getting to know the right people in the right place at the right time.

So think of a fashion career as a show-business pursuit. That way, you will not be too easily jaded or disappointed. If you are timid, look elsewhere. Nerves of steel and intense drive are two key ingredients to success.

Starting Out

A career in fashion may seem to be an overwhelming undertaking. But with preparation and steady reality checks, it's really quite manageable. This book gives a comprehensive overview of career options that suit your individual skills. Not everyone can be icons such as Donna Karan or Issey Miyake, so we've described a range of career choices that includes clothing and accessory designer, fabric maker, theatrical dresser, buyer, fashion show organizer, boutique owner, store window artist, makeup consultant, fashion journalist, teacher, photographer, model, and more.

One of the most appealing aspects of the fashion business is its constant need for top-notch talent. Whether you receive the bulk of your training through an accredited design school program or learn on the job as an apprentice, your unique creativity and business savvy will be your greatest assets.

The Internet has placed fashion publications, discussion groups, and information on industry events around the world at your fingertips. Schools that offer internships and design competitions are geared toward your individual needs and interests. A wealth of fashion-related associations and organizations—such as New York–based Fashion Group International and the Canadian Apparel Federation—are excellent forums for networking and learning firsthand about this glamorous but highly demanding profession (see Appendix A for professional organizations and schools in both the United States and Canada).

Most important, fashion is a people industry. Your ability to communicate clearly and effectively will set you apart from less-assertive individuals hoping to break into fashion's tight-knit inner circle.

Beyond skill, education, and confidence comes a willingness to keep your name and your work in the public eye—or, at least, in the eyes of influential fashion professionals who can help move your career ahead. Despite all the technological advancements in the world of design, it is still very much an area that relies on mentors and one-on-one guidance. For example, if going to a party thrown by the editor of *Vogue* would allow you to meet some key people, by all means be there. This applies not only to designers, but also to fashion photographers, journalists, models, and others.

You must constantly stay abreast of trends and social changes that may influence the way people dress. Endless curiosity and astute observation skills are crucial to succeeding in the field.

Also be aware that certain cities—New York, Los Angeles, Toronto, London, Milan, Paris, and Tokyo—are fashion capitals. Your chances of success in these places could be viewed two ways. Working in these cities would expose you to some of the most powerful trendsetters in the business; yet, because those markets are already saturated, you may drown in a sea of fashion wannabes. So it is up to you to decide how confident you are about your work and skills and how happy and comfortable you would be working in these cities. Of course, you could pursue your fashion career almost anywhere in the world—even create a new style capital if you are that driven. What counts is your personal satisfaction, earning a living in the field, and sharing your talents with consumers from all walks of life.

Are You Fashion Material?

Before pursuing fashion—a profession that will undoubtedly consume your life—you should ask yourself some basic questions about your suitability for such a demanding career. Simply liking to sew or sketch creative ideas is not enough to land you consistent work. But knowing what is expected of you in a realistic business sense will set you on the right footing.

Now, before stepping onto your career "runway," make sure you are not going to misstep. Ask yourself these questions to see if your qualifications are a match for the fashion industry.

1. Are you willing to spend long hours doing tedious manual work?
2. Can you be creative while knowing what styles will sell in various consumer markets?
3. Do you like to take risks?
4. Are you ultraconfident that you bring unique skills to the field?
5. Are you an avid follower of fashion trends?
6. Does travel appeal to you?
7. Do you have a competitive, driven personality?
8. Are you interested in the fine arts?
9. Do you react well to criticism?
10. Can you actively and consistently promote yourself?

Now review your reactions in light of some specifics on each question.

Most fashion designers are also tailors and seamsters who not only create but also cut out their own patterns. Although use of computerized sewing machines is now a given, hand stitching and other intricate custom work are still in demand. This is one area in which old-world ways of making garments are highly regarded in an industry whose major selling point is quality.

Whether you are a designer or a fashion publicist, it is critical to apply your creative outbursts wisely. Thigh-high patent leather boots and fishnet halter tops make for great magazine photo ops, but will these items sell at major retail chains? Knowing your market can mean the difference between creating modern art clothes that don't sell and designing beautifully structured ensembles that bring you both substantial income and a sought-after reputation.

Taking risks is inevitable in this unpredictable arena, where styles breeze by as quickly as the seasons. If you opt to own your own boutique or open a fashion photography studio, be prepared to cover your overhead costs and know how to most effectively sell your services.

Don't settle for anything less than being confident that you can bring something different to the table. During interviews with fashion magazine editors, wholesalers, and other industry professionals, you will be asked what sets you apart from others. In a business perpetually looking for new trends, think of ways you can get an edge on originality.

If you have a passion for new styles, you are certainly fashion material. Being design conscious and loving clothes and accessories are positive signs that you will be happy in this profession. Enjoying a change of scene also bodes well. Fashion is international and very mobile, so you will be required to travel frequently.

To say competition is fierce in this business is a gross understatement. It is downright brutal at times, and you should be aware of that up front. Therefore, you must consistently remain on top of things by being competitive and driven.

Because fashion is a form of art, your attention to detail, beauty, and quality are imperative to your success. Approach your career as an artist would. Refine your talents and develop a meticulous eye for detail.

Like any highly visible, showy occupation, fashion promotes an open forum for criticism and debate. Fashion editors determine 90 percent of style trends, and design professionals are constantly reviewed in a critical light. Know this. Expect it. And learn how to take constructive criticism to improve your craft.

You must feel comfortable with drawing attention to yourself. Because you *are* your work, self-promotion is vital to your continuing popularity. This industry is filled with enormous egos, and, as self-serving as it sounds, you will need one, too, in order to survive and be noticed.

But don't let all this competitive talk get you down. If you are determined to have a successful fashion career—and there are so many areas from which to choose—you will. Not only is it an exciting, quick-paced industry, it is one whose creative energy and theatrical bravura are unrivaled in the more traditional business world.

A Sampling of Fashion Careers

Now we will see which category best suits your talents and interests. The opportunities are endless, and if you decide to move from, say, fashion design to fashion teaching or photography, you can make a smooth transition. All segments of the industry intersect—so set your sights high from the start, and you will be on the right track.

Careers in Clothing Design

Most fashion designers specialize in either womenswear or menswear. This makes it much easier to market designs to a specific group and allows one to find a comfortable niche in which to hone creative skills. There are also professionals who choose to design exclusively for children.

As a designer, you will be required to sketch, cut out patterns, select fabric, and sew, as well as coordinate garments you wish to display in a fashion show. Most high-fashion designers are self-employed and design for individual clients or cater to specialty and department stores. Long hours are the norm in design, and self-promotion is a key way of getting noticed.

Other positions in this field include fabric designers, seamsters, and tailors. Fabric designers hold degrees in textile arts or learn on the job with weavers and other fiber specialists. Seamsters and tailors, who do everything from custom sewing to complex garment alterations, are also critical to this particular area's growth and stability.

Careers in Accessory Design

Many clothing designers also create accessories for women, men, and children. Items typically include handbags or cases, scarves, gloves, hats, shoes, jewelry and watches, cosmetics, fragrances, eyewear, belts, buttons, hair accessories, ties, and much more. An object that complements or "finishes" an outfit is considered an accessory.

But, unlike fashion designers, accessory artists don't necessarily need to know how to sew or cut patterns. Instead, this profession requires intricate, highly specialized handwork—such as soldering and gluing—and drawing talents. Accessory artists are typically self-employed and design for individual customers or sell their pieces to boutiques and large apparel stores.

Careers in Performing Arts and Specialty Apparel Design

For those creative folks who have a love for the arts or other unique categories, these are fun markets that require one to be well versed in other subjects. For example, if designing for the stage, knowledge of theater arts is crucial. By combining work as an actor or director with costume design, you have an edge over the competition by simply knowing the nuances of scene changes and stage blocking. Dancewear designers must be knowledgeable about a performer's anatomy, as well as understand proper materials and fitting for shoes.

The area of specialty apparel includes all sporting attire, as well as uniforms and special-occasion garments such as bridal, graduation, and religious apparel. A little-known segment of the performing arts is that of the professional dresser for the theater. This occupation involves helping performers with their costume changes and making alterations on the spot backstage.

Careers in Wholesale and Retail Sales

The business side of fashion encompasses a wide range of professions, including buyers, sales representatives, trade show and event organizers, boutique owners, window and countertop display artists, and fashion publicists.

Some of these are behind-the-scenes jobs that get the trends off the ground and out into the consumer arena. Most of these people set the style pace as they buy and sell on trade-show floors and runways around the world. They work long hours, travel extensively, and require polished sales and textile-related backgrounds.

Careers in Fashion Writing and Photography

As mentioned earlier, fashion journalists ultimately determine what is in style by the articles and photos they run. They are at the big design shows and report to the global community what's hot in the industry. Less trendsetting writing jobs include copywriters for catalogs and mail-order houses. These writers, incidentally, are usually freelancers who work out of their homes on their personal computers.

Fashion photographers are in great demand, both on the runways and in studios doing millions of dollars' worth of advertising photography. They also photograph aspiring models for composites and portfolio material. Some fashion photographers work exclusively with certain well-known designers.

Careers in Fashion Education

Most top designers have completed an accredited course in fashion design, and there are numerous top-notch design schools around the world. If you are a designer with a talent for instructing future trendsetters in the field, a teaching career could be quite rewarding. Positions also are available in the textile departments of high schools, colleges, and universities. A flexible teaching schedule would allow you to pursue your individual designing career while passing your knowledge on to others.

Besides teaching, you can apply your fashion know-how as a fashion or makeup consultant. Consultants work in the corporate sector, in boutiques, in theater and film, and at the cosmetics counters of department stores. Clothing and makeup stylists are professionals who set up fashion shots for print media and television. They dress models and help determine proper camera angles and lighting.

Careers in Modeling

High-fashion modeling remains one of the most competitive sides of the business. Everyone is attracted to the glamour, celebrity, and big bucks. But only a handful really make it—as in Hollywood. To reach the top of this field, models need a combination of talent, beauty, poise, street smarts, timing, and business savvy.

It is, therefore, very important to know what to look for in a reputable modeling or talent agency and how to put together a winning portfolio. It's also essential to be aware of the full scope of the modeling world. Runway modeling is only one aspect of the field. Other areas to consider are steady modeling work for catalogs and corporate videos as well as specialty modeling, which involves showing only certain body parts, such as hands, feet, and legs, for product shots involving jewelry, shoes, and hosiery.

This book will help point you in the right direction by providing critical tips that will give you a realistic picture of the appealing, glitzy, wild world of fashion.

CHAPTER TWO

Creating for the Runway: Clothing Design

Bravo TV's megahit "Project Runway" has no doubt inspired a whole new crop of clothing designers. Despite its overwrought drama and catfights, the reality show offers viewers a rare and pretty accurate insider look into the world of fashion. It also draws attention to the importance of a designer crafting his or her original artistic voice, together with the practical sides of the business and the need for excellent training. The various projects—from designing a dress out of flowers and plants to making a costume for a figure-skating champion—are great challenges for aspiring designers to try for themselves. Overall, the program gives a broader sense of the design process and encompasses models, makeup artists, fashion journalists, and instructors all aiming, in the words of the program's beloved style mentor, Tim Gunn, to "make it work."

So, a combination of talent, timing, creativity, and great networking skills are the main ingredients for a successful career as a clothing designer. Many professionals in this field specialize in certain markets, such as womenswear, menswear, and children's attire, in order to focus their efforts and better manage their innovative ideas. They most commonly work for apparel manufacturers and adapt men's, women's, and children's fashions for the mass market. A large segment of fashion designers are self-employed and design for individual clients. They essentially create a "line" of clothes for each season—working at least two seasons ahead—by defining cut, colors, fabrics, and hemlines. Other high-fashion designers cater to specialty stores or upscale department stores.

Your duties as a clothing designer will encompass many disciplines, including sketching, pattern making, and sewing. Rarely will you work regular nine-to-five days. Because you are an artist, your mind is constantly generating ideas, so there are no time limits to how long or exactly when you work. During the busiest times, when new collections are unveiled for spring/summer and fall/winter seasons, you could work around the clock.

Designers do not carry their projects from start to finish single-handedly; they spark the process that begins with an idea and goes to a sketch, to a sample, and to mass production. As an example of how the various segments of fashion overlap, copies of the garment go from the fashion model to the store buyer and, ultimately, to the consumer.

Womenswear Designers

Based on an informal survey of fifty designers around the United States, eight out of ten prefer to design exclusively for women. Why? Because women's fashions change more frequently than men's, offer more creative latitude, and attract consumers who generally change and update their wardrobes with each season. More fabric choices and items are also available. In recent years, designers have favored hazy pastels, cool industrial hues, and organic fabrics. Styles have ranged from re-creations of swinging London of the 1960s to corset-inspired dresses and glam gowns with theatrical flair.

The statistics don't lie. Take some of the most famous designers—such as Isaac Mizrahi, Laura Biagiotti, Vera Wang, Geoffrey Beene, Yves Saint Laurent, Hussein Chalayan, and Dorothy Grant—whose womenswear collections have generated million-dollar empires. They, too, prefer the endless variety of trendsetting opportunities.

As a designer for women, you can streamline your work even more by specializing in a subcategory, such as sportswear, career apparel, evening attire, knitwear, coats and jackets (leather, fabric, fur), lingerie and hosiery, sleepwear and swimwear, sweaters, or casual separates.

Casual separates design is one of the most popular areas because many women work at home or in jobs that don't require the traditional corporate navy blue suit. Practical separates, which allow one's wardrobe to be mixed and matched, move quite easily from day to evening and fit women's changing lifestyles.

Menswear Designers

Although most designers prefer to create appealing clothes for women, there is also a big market for menswear styles. In fact, because womenswear is so popular among designers, it might not be a bad idea to explore the somewhat less crowded, but highly meticulous, world of men's ensembles.

Since Giorgio Armani relaxed the shoulders of men's jackets, making "unstructured" one of the longest-lasting buzz words in the industry, menswear designers have gotten bolder. They still design high-quality linen, wool, and cotton suits, but they are no longer restricted to conservative solid colors, such as black, blue, and gray. A quick glance at the red carpet during the Academy Awards reveals many creative takes on suits and tuxedos—from daring primary colors and patterns to long-cut jackets and world-inspired fabrics. Yet, overall, menswear remains a steady market, where colors and cuts may vary but the essential garments remain the same. Famous designers, such as Calvin Klein, Ralph Lauren, and Givenchy, have made fortunes from their impeccably con-structed lines that run from formal to business to casual wear.

Because professional men tend to buy ensembles that will last a long time, menswear designers should be attentive to a garment's durability and quality. Areas in which you can focus are custom-tailored suits, shirts and slacks, coats and jackets (leather, fabric, fur), sportswear, sweaters, casual separates, sleepwear and swimwear, and undergarments.

While a number of menswear designers work with individual clients, most are employed with large design-manufacturing firms, where they work as part of a team.

Children's Clothing Designers

If you want to turn your attention to a less popular, but very lucrative, side of the business, consider designing clothes for children. Department stores and specialty boutiques are always looking to fill their children's departments with colorful, eye-catching garments. While you will probably work for a major manufacturer, there are opportunities to build your own clientele and eventually open your own store. Categories for children's garments include play clothes and sportswear, party outfits, sleepwear and swimwear, and underwear.

Although there are not as many fashion shows featuring children's clothing, you can still market your merchandise to major apparel centers and larger stores. Knowing what is cool for the kiddie set is a definite asset. You may want to talk with moms, dads, and preschool or elementary teachers, watch a lot of children's TV programs, and go to the latest youth-oriented movies to find out what kids like to wear.

On the latter subject, merchandising from films and television shows continues to be a hot marketing phenomenon. If you could hook up with a major children's company, such as Disney or Warner Brothers, you would enjoy steady work and a career with promising growth opportunities. There are also many other channels in which to become a success. Kids' clothes are always in demand. Don't underestimate the options available in this challenging, but less competitive, design field.

Fabric Designers

As you delve deeper into the clothing design profession, you will notice that there are even more highly specialized areas. Fabric design is one of them. In this field, you must be an expert in weaving, dyeing materials, sewing, or knitting. Working with processed cottons, wools, and silk strands—to name a few raw materials— you would be employed either at a large manufacturing firm or with your own independent company.

Technology has made the process much easier through advanced machinery, such as computerized looms and cutters. For the most part, however, expertise in textiles, fibers, and the proper treatment of materials is essential to rising to the top of the industry.

Fashion designers rely on your ideas for color and print combinations. If you enjoy developing patterns and imagery on cloth, this select profession is one that is highly prized. Fabric designers are perpetually in demand, as long as couturiers use material— whether it is cloth, vinyl, or plastic—for their creations.

Because fashion designers are becoming increasingly conscious of our world's fragile environment, many designers work only with earth-friendly fabrics. These "green" designers prefer organically grown fibers and recyclable materials. For instance, British designer Georgina Goodman fashions dressy high-heeled shoes out of recycled soda cans for a funky yet elegant look. You may want to take some time exploring the scientific side of fibers and certain materials that, when discarded, don't pollute the environment. It's one major step toward making our planet healthier while giving fashion a higher purpose.

Seamsters and Tailors

The textile industry offers employment opportunities in a variety of occupations, but production occupations account for 64 percent of all jobs and encompass seamsters and tailors. Because designers rely on these specialists to piece together their garment ideas in solid form, they are crucial to the overall fashion industry. Working in factories, modern manufacturing facilities, laundries, and dry cleaners, they typically rotate shifts on a standard five-day, thirty-five- to forty-hour week.

Because of the value and delicate nature of some materials, sewing may be done by hand rather than on a machine—although machines, and increasingly high-tech ones, are the norm. As a highly skilled hand sewer, you would specialize in a particular area, such as embroidery or sewing on lace and other trims. You might also work with a designer to make a sample of a new product.

When sewing operations have been completed, workers remove loose threads, basting stitching, and lint from the finished product. Final inspection may be done at this time.

Another highly skilled career track within this area is that of custom tailor. Custom tailors make garments from start to finish, including taking measurements and selecting fabrics, and they must be knowledgeable about all phases of clothing production. Many tailors work in retail outlets, where they make alterations and adjustments to ready-to-wear clothing.

Getting Started

Here are a few tips on how to get your start in fashion design.

Clothing and Fabric Designers

If you are efficient at meeting tight deadlines and have confidence in your ability to invent a new look or style, start preparing for a design career as early as high school. Your high school home economics department typically offers courses in textiles and sewing. Take them, along with art and general business classes, to get a lead on the competition. Keep honing your computer skills to gain a facility with machines and learn about new design techniques for the twenty-first century.

Working part-time at a boutique or fabric store will put you in touch with the local design community and help you master the industry's terminology. To stay abreast of changing styles, and what social conditions usually prompt them, keep a file of designs you have cut out of fashion magazines or create a folder on your PC. Then set aside sufficient time to practice your sketching skills because most designers are also artists who put their ideas down on paper before getting out the scissors.

Other ways to begin include assisting local organizations with their annual fashion shows and visiting textile and art museums. Fashion shows will familiarize you with how a runway show is put together, and they will give you an aesthetic sense of quality fabrics and lines. Visiting museums will give you a historical perspective that may influence your future designs.

When you are ready to pursue a design degree or become a designer's apprentice, you will be that far ahead of the fashion game. In fact, moving to one of the key fashion centers of the world would immerse you in the vigorous pace of this dynamic industry. The Seventh Avenue garment district in New York City, despite the area's ongoing transformation, has been historically regarded as the U.S. fashion capital for its concentration of manufacturers, designers, showrooms, and schools. California produces a high number of sportswear designers. Many Canadian designers work with various fabrics and raw materials (such as wool, fur, and leather) indigenous to particular provinces, such as Quebec and Newfoundland. Fashion designers also work for American companies that produce garments overseas. These companies often require their designers to travel extensively to Asia,

Europe, and South America to review the development of first samples—the prototypes of products to be manufactured.

Seamsters and Tailors

In addition to all fabric creators and designers for men, women, and children, the above suggestions apply to seamsters and tailors, who are directly involved in the overall design process. Educating themselves about design issues will pay off.

Education and Training

There are a variety ways to learn your craft. Here are suggestions for gaining the skills you need for various clothing design careers.

Clothing and Fabric Designers

You may not need a formal degree to succeed as a fashion designer—especially if you're a sartorial genius with a sharp knack for networking and self-promotion. In this case, simply teaming up with an influential designer as an apprentice or getting some hands-on experience in retail might be sufficient. Taking classes, and even completing a design program, would certainly increase your knowledge of textiles, fabrics, ornamentation, and trends. A degree, however, is essential to a fabric designer.

There now exist approximately 250 postsecondary institutions with programs in art and design accredited by the National Association of Schools of Art and Design. Most of these schools award a degree in fashion design. Many schools do not allow formal entry into a program until a student has successfully finished basic art and design courses. Applicants may be required to submit sketches and other examples of artistic ability.

Two- or four-year degree programs in fine arts exist throughout the United States and Canada, as well as two- and three-year professional schools that award certificates or associate's degrees in design. Graduates of two-year programs generally qualify as assistants to designers. An ideal curriculum would include courses in art history, sketching, life (anatomical) drawing, garment construction, draping, pattern making, textiles, and merchandising. A few schools offer one-year programs in practical design. Studies stress applied skills rather than liberal arts courses.

The Fashion Institute of Technology and Parsons The New School for Design, both in New York City, are among the most sought out and respected fashion educational institutions in the United States. Contact the schools if you are curious about their programs (see Appendix A). They can provide you with course catalogs and sample programs to suit your interests.

When selecting a school, visit the campus and talk with faculty members to determine if a particular program will sufficiently prepare you for a career in fashion or fabric design. Try to talk with students, too. Often, they can give you insights that you wouldn't find in the printed promotional materials the schools provide. Remember to check the status of the school; it should be in good standing with one or more accrediting associations.

Remember, too, that many prestigious design programs exist across Canada and Europe. The International Academy of Design and Technology in Toronto, Ontario, offers an intensive two-year course of study in fashion design. The program is aimed at preparing graduates for a career in the design, creation, and marketing of fashion. In the first year, students are introduced to the development and construction of apparel, the fundamentals of design, and the sourcing and use of textiles. The second year, the program combines these hands-on skills with a variety of creative design projects. Students are also introduced to the commercial side of the fashion-design world, as well as to industry-standard computer applications. Graduates have the opportunity to enter the job market with a professional portfolio that can include apparel for men and women.

Italy, France, and the United Kingdom all boast highly respected fashion education institutions. Paris is France's design capital, and most of Italy's academies are located in Milan and Rome. Interestingly, Florence's Polimoda Fashion School offers a course in conjunction with New York's Fashion Institute of Technology for two to four years, with a three-year Italian language study program.

As an example of a growing high-tech international design school, let's take a look at the London College of Fashion, which is part of the University of the Arts London, a federation of six prestigious art and design colleges that also include Camberwell College of Arts, Central Saint Martins College of Art and Design, Chelsea College of Art and Design, London College of Communication, and Wimbledon College of Art.

In addition to workrooms, design studios, and lecture theaters, the college has a fashion theater with a permanent catwalk; video suites, radio facilities, and photographic studios geared toward fashion promotion work; extensive computer rooms; a multimedia facility; wet and dry textile testing labs; specialist makeup and body treatment salons; a teaching gymnasium for health, beauty, and modeling work; a cosmetics lab; foreign language studies areas; extensive sample and production workrooms; and a comprehensive fashion library. Many other programs like this exist. You can find them through fashion design associations or by asking your guidance or career counselors. Most of these schools have their own websites.

Seamsters and Tailors

While seamsters and tailors within the apparel industry do not need formal education to enter the field or climb the fashion ladder, they should be aware of the high-tech equipment used to sew garments. In addition, most of their education takes place on the job, where they are commonly assigned to a mentor who instructs by demonstration. Practice, ultimately, is the best training for seamsters and tailors.

Operators of large textile machinery will be better prepared if they've taken courses in computer technology. Staying informed about changes in technology-advanced manufacturing methods is essential in this branch of the fashion industry. Energy, stamina, meticulous attention to detail, and dexterity also are necessary skills. Today, a high school diploma and extensive technical training are becoming entry requirements. Technical schools provide this type of hands-on instruction, as do manufacturers with reliable training programs.

In fact, training is one form of advancement, with some workers becoming instructors and training new employees. Others progress by taking positions requiring more advanced skills and greater responsibility. First-line supervisory positions usually are filled from the ranks of skilled operators.

Where the Jobs Are

We'll explore ways of finding a job in this competitive field.

Clothing and Fabric Designers and Apparel Manufacturers

A winning portfolio of sketches and designs is a key selling point when looking for a job in clothing or fabric design. Major design schools will be able to point you in the right direction regarding entry-level positions—such as assistants and display coordinators—and your local apparel center is a popular job source. If you ask fashion designers how they got a foot in the door, they will frequently tell you they worked in a boutique or dry cleaner doing alterations to learn more about the construction of garments, then teamed up with a designer mentor who guided them along their career paths.

Participation in charity fashion shows gets your name out, and if members of the press attend, they will be the first to unveil your talents to the public. Getting to know fashion editors from your city's daily and weekly newspapers is a big plus. Sending resumes to department stores and successfully interviewing with portfolio in hand will get you into larger fashion centers that could give you invaluable design and retail experience.

As in most fields, networking can be the key to the job hunt. Research can also help. Career sections of libraries provide a directory of fashion companies you can target. The Internet is a huge job resource (see Appendix A for fashion associations and their websites).

Apparel workers such as seamsters and tailors work primarily in department stores and large manufacturing firms. They fill out application forms and, if their applications are accepted, are invited to have interviews. Scanning the classified ads in your local newspaper or online, or registering with a reputable job search firm, will point you in the right direction.

Marketing Yourself

As discussed earlier, the world of fashion design is fiercely competitive. So, you must be equally talented at setting fashion trends and at promoting yourself. One important method is through the print and electronic media. To let the media know that you're an up-and-coming designer, send out print and online media kits on your recent collections or a fashion show you organized.

Entering design competitions is an excellent way to show the fashion universe that you mean business. The Arts of Fashion International Design Competition is one example. A panel of judges selects forty to sixty finalists from about four hundred entries from around the globe. The chosen finalists then construct two of their designs to be shown at the annual fashion forum, where another round of judging determines two award winners in the accessories category and six winners in fashion design.

Market yourself over the Internet. Technology on the Internet has exploded, and fashion is a highly visible force in this field. Many designers have their own blogs, join fashion chat groups from their personal computers, and can upload photographs and video clips of their designs to show the world.

One popular and up-to-date Web fashion zine is Fashionline (www.fashionline.org), which includes articles and information on fashion fairs and auctions and provides space for designers to post announcements.

Seamsters and tailors, who focus on the production side of fashion, are not required to vigorously promote themselves. Therefore, positions in this field are quite straightforward. Most skilled workers can find positions made known through help wanted ads and word of mouth.

Opportunities and Earnings

The following salary outlooks reveal the field's ongoing changes.

Clothing and Fabric Designers

Fashion design is a small field; there are approximately seventeen thousand fashion designers in the United States. Salaries vary depending on market swings and how popular your designs are. Clothing designers earned an average of $55,840 per year in 2004. Besides the benefits that accompany any high-profile job, as a designer you will get to travel, set your own hours, and be fairly independent—and the potential to earn millions does exist. A few well-known designers in top firms can earn from $60,000 to $100,000 a year or more. They may become partners in the firms for which they design apparel. Most entry-level design assistant and design room worker positions pay, on average, $500 a week.

Remember that this is an intensely competitive field. The number of people who try to get into top designing is always greater than the number of job openings. Yet there are opportunities for those with talent, skill, perseverance, and relentless business savvy. Overall, employment of fashion designers is projected to grow more slowly than the average for all occupations through 2014. The best job opportunities will be in design firms that design mass market clothing sold in department and retail chain stores.

Seamsters and Tailors

One out of three textile industry jobs are concentrated in North Carolina, South Carolina, and Georgia. In 2004, 416,000 workers were employed in the textile mills and textile product industries, while 285,000 worked in the apparel manufacturing industry. According to the U.S. Bureau of Labor Statistics, seamsters and tailors earned a median hourly wage of $10.79 in 2004, with weekly earnings that averaged between $351 and $443, depending upon their places of employment.

Aside from employer-sponsored benefits, some workers derive benefits from membership in UNITE HERE, a union that represents more than 450,000 active members in the apparel and textile industries, laundries, casinos, hotels, and food-service sectors.

The job outlook for apparel workers depends largely on conditions in the apparel industry. Job opportunities in cut-and-sew manufacturing will continue to decline as apparel is increasingly manufactured overseas. Most companies employ in-house fashion designers, however. Increased imports, use of offshore assembly, and heightened productivity resulting from automation are expected to reduce demand for these workers. Employment of apparel workers is expected to decline by 46 percent through 2014. Nevertheless, some job openings will arise from the need to replace persons who transfer to other occupations or retire.

Opportunities look most promising for custom tailors and pressing machine operators. Retail establishments, laundries, and dry cleaners employ many of these workers. These employers are unaffected by imports and are unable to move operations abroad. Because companies in certain locations are having difficulty attracting enough of these skilled workers, those workers with the appropriate qualifications and background should find ample opportunities.

Most textile machinery operators are employed in weaving, finishing, and yarn and thread mills. Other employers include knitting mills and manufactured fiber producers. North Carolina has been the leading state in the employment of textile workers, accounting for approximately 15 percent of the total. Georgia and South Carolina combined account for another 18 percent. Most of the remaining workers are employed in California and the Northeast.

CHAPTER THREE

Pursuing Accessory Design

A gourmet baker wouldn't leave a wedding cake unfrosted, and rarely would an interior designer make room for just the furniture and ignore crucial accoutrements like rugs, vases, and visual art. Therefore, fashion designers seldom neglect the embellishments that put the finishing touches on an outfit. Enter accessory designers. Employed in a vast array of subcategories within the fashion arena, they make up a much-needed cache of experts in jewelry, shoe, hat, and belt making, to name just a few areas. Like fashion designers, accessory designers specialize in products for women, children, or men. The smallest specialty is the design of children's accessories.

Many accessory designers are self-employed and design for individual customers or sell their wares to boutiques and large apparel stores. Among the items considered accessories are jewelry, handbags and cases, scarves, gloves, hats, ties, shoes, eyewear and sunglasses, belts, hair accessories, and buttons. Although many of these items can be mass produced, there still exists a need for special, handmade accessories.

This is especially true in the popular field of jewelry. For instance, you may be employed at a large firm that utilizes your innovative design talents through sketching and even building a ring, bracelet, or necklace. If you choose to focus on a particular ethnic or modern geometric style, your designs may prove quite valuable. You will find that you can sell your pieces as if they were miniature works of art.

If you have acquired expertise in fashioning leather for belts and purses or making hats, there are endless opportunities for you to work from your home, at a specialty store, or for a major design company. Incidentally, many clothing designers cross over into the accessory realm.

Like a fashion designer, you can't expect to work regular hours, unless you work on-site at an accessory firm. Because accessory design is not as competitive as the clothing arena, you will not participate in such a grueling fashion show schedule, accompanied by intense self-promotion. You will, however, still be engaged in major networking activity, primarily through industry trade shows, art fairs, and one-on-one meetings with store owners. On the job, you will be involved in sketching, metalworking, and fabric styling, depending upon which specific area you choose.

Women's and Children's Accessories

Women accessorize more than men, so it is not surprising that women's accessory design is a popular field. A small niche market for children's accessories, such as belts and hair clips, also exists. Designing accessories for children is often a side career that individuals choose to complement, for example, their clothing designs for the youth set.

While clothing designs change from season to season, accessories often have greater staying power, which is one of the reasons accessory designers are regarded as artists. A diamond ring, for example, could be a cherished heirloom that might be passed from generation to generation. While adapting your designs to current market demands, you are working with a wealth of high-quality materials that tend to outlast trends.

This doesn't mean that accessory designers can ignore trends. Clothing styles influence accessories. If you are going to succeed in the consumer marketplace, you must know what's hot in clothing styles so that you can create embellishments that will sell.

Both costume and precious jewelry design are among the most popular accessory design careers. Jewelers use gold, diamonds, silver, bronze, and other metals and precious gems to make, repair, and adjust rings, necklaces, bracelets, earrings, and other jewelry. Along with chemicals and polishing compounds, they use a variety of tools and materials, such as drills, pliers, soldering torches, saws, and other implements, to mold metal and set gemstones.

The precise nature of this work naturally demands finger and hand dexterity, good hand-eye coordination, patience, and concentration. Not only will you design a piece, but you will most likely make the piece as well. Artistic imagination and attention to detail are what set successful jewelry designers apart.

Other areas require certain technical skills. For example, hat design (millinery) demands skills in hat blocking, pattern cutting, and trimming. Shoemaking is a craft unto itself, in which up-and-coming designers do intense training sessions with a master craftsperson. Here, familiarity with the foot's anatomy is crucial.

Men's Accessories

Men's accessories are not as varied as women's, but they are in consistent demand. Take ties, for instance. They often represent a man's personality, and some professionals custom order ties from specialty designers.

Belts are another popular area in which skills in leather treatment and cutting are necessary. Leather working can also be used for items such as wallets and briefcases. Sunglasses and eyewear are other important categories, where large firms employ their own frame designers to keep up with this constantly busy market.

Jewelry is as highly regarded among men as it is among women, only on a more streamlined scale (rings, chains, and bracelets). Men tend to buy fewer items, but they are concerned with quality. When men buy jewelry, it is meant to last a very long time.

The skills required are the same across the field of accessory design. Successful designers pay careful attention to men's clothing fashions. In addition, an understanding of the male physique and psyche can help you break into this specialized business.

Getting Started

A sensible way to determine where you fit in the accessory spectrum is to take basic art courses in high school that will give you a good foundation for the field. Because very few educational institutions offer specific degrees in leather crafting or jewelry making, you will probably find yourself majoring in art, fine arts, metalworking, or even fashion design. Textiles are also used in this area, so familiarize yourself with fabrics at stores or at a textile museum. (Many cities have them.) These same places occasionally offer workshops in design and arts and crafts.

Become an avid fashion watcher to get a feel for the popular clothes that would match your accessory designs. Hook up with a local boutique that has a market for unusual accessories—items that will help you hone your own individual style. At a specialty store, you can share your sketches with the owner and ask questions to show your keen interest in the field. By doing this, you may come in contact with master craftspeople, one of whom could invite you to become an apprentice.

At home, see how creative you can be by rummaging through odds and ends to use in an accessory-making project. You might make your own earrings or purse with raw materials at hand. Because many accessories are ethnically based, research different cultures to learn about unique materials and techniques for creating garment embellishments. Then test the interest in your designs by marketing them at local craft stores or art fairs.

By using these strategies, you will narrow the field considerably and determine where you excel in the eclectic accessory arena.

Once you've selected your niche, you can begin to learn the specialized skills that will help you succeed. Whatever you select, you will need a strong personal sense of style to make one-of-a-kind creations plus strong marketing skills to sell your first designs.

....

Education and Training

As in clothing design, no formal education is required, but it is highly recommended. According to the National Association of Schools of Art and Design, there are approximately 250 institutions with art and design programs. Most of these schools award a degree in art as opposed to a specific accessory field. Courses are available in specific disciplines, however, such as hat design or leather working.

Some people are naturally talented and hone their crafts through one-on-one lessons with a mentor. They can advance by consistently producing unique, high-quality items that attract the discerning eyes of store owners and individual clients. Most accessory specialists agree that repetitious practice of the craft is the best way to learn.

One particular field that receives a lot of attention in the accessory arena is jewelry. Jewelers, who hold about forty-two thousand jobs in the United States, often learn their skills in technical schools, correspondence courses, or on-the-job training. Some begin working as clerks in department stores and transfer to jobs in jewelry shops or manufacturing firms after gaining experience. Those who want further education may pursue a bachelor's or master's degree in fine arts from a school of art and design. Formal training in the basic skills of the trade enhances employment and advancement opportunities. Many employers prefer well-rounded jewelers with design, repair, and sales skills.

To enter most technical school or college programs, a high school diploma or its equivalent is required. Courses in art, math, mechanical drawing, and chemistry are useful. Because computer-aided design is increasingly used in the jewelry field, computer studies are highly recommended.

In jewelry manufacturing plants, workers have traditionally developed their skills through on-the-job training programs, which may last three to four years. Training usually focuses on casting, stone setting, model making, or engraving. Those who are interested in manufacturing should be skilled at computer-aided design.

Another fashion accessory occupation is that of shoe and leather workers. Many are self-employed individuals who own and operate small shoe shops or specialty leather manufacturing firms. Others are employed in the manufacture of footwear products or leather goods, such as luggage, handbags, and apparel.

Once again, most precision shoe and leather workers learn their crafts on the job, either through in-house training programs or by working as helpers to experienced employees. Helpers begin by performing simple tasks and then progress to more difficult projects, such as cutting or stitching leather. Trainees can become fully skilled in six months to two years.

A limited number of schools offer vocational training in shoe repair and leather work. These programs, which may last from six months to one year, focus on leather cutting, stitching, and dyeing. Students learn shoe construction, practice shoe repair, and study the fundamentals of running a small business.

Continuing education and specialized skills are important. Experienced employees may participate in continuing education by attending special seminars to keep up with the latest trends in the industry. Those in manufacturing usually seek training in computer skills as well.

Besides being attuned to the individual style needs of women, children, and men, accessory students overall are not required to narrow their work to a specific gender or age group. Once they have attained basic, specialized skills, they can concentrate on designing for any group or market niche. The same skills apply in diverse areas. Those interested in this field will need manual dexterity and a sense of style. They should also expect to face a difficult job market.

Where the Jobs Are

One of the best sources for job opportunities in accessory design is your local apparel center or others throughout the country. Design schools can also point you in the right direction, recommending manufacturing firms and specialty stores. You should search fashion sites on the Internet. Most of your job hunting will, however, depend on your exceptional skills and ability to market your products. Starting out in a small jewelry store, for example, would provide much-needed experience before branching out to the larger arena.

By applying to specialty stores or accessory departments of large shopping centers, you can gain a firm footing in the business. From this point, your options expand. You now have access to industry professionals who may like your work and recommend other employment opportunities.

Self-Marketing Opportunities

Despite the number of options available in this burgeoning field, you should not let your guard down and think that finding a job is easy. Many people aspire to enter this field, so you will face competition. In fact, if you choose to be your own boss, you will have to work doubly hard at promoting yourself—perhaps not as intensely as a fashion designer would, but with drive and determination nonetheless.

Touting your products to boutiques and larger department stores is a challenge that involves stamina, innovation, and a firm grip on handling rejection and/or criticism. Even after you have established yourself, you still must work to maintain high standards and get the word out about your designs. No matter how long you have been in business, you still must produce a consistently original, high-quality accessory, whether it's a tie, hat, handbag, or piece of jewelry. A good example of innovative design is Italian sculptor and designer Sandra Di Giacinto's Plissé bag collection. Influenced by Japanese art and constructed of recycled materials, her purse can be assembled into different shapes so that it is really several bags in one.

Attending industry trade shows and art fairs will put you in touch with accessory professionals on all levels. If you can afford a booth or stand at these events, your chances of being noticed will be even greater. Exposing yourself to other designers is a great way to size up your competition. By seeing other designers' work exhibited in one large area, you will get a quick overview of some of the top-selling items.

In addition, you should speak with fashion show organizers who may be interested in pairing and featuring your accessories with clothes. They probably won't pay you initially, but your product will get some terrific free advertising. Such fashion show contacts can lead to other more lucrative employment opportunities in this variety-filled design profession. And who knows? You could become a household name by accident. Think of what the HBO series "Sex and the City" did for Manolo Blahnik shoes.

Opportunities and Earnings

The personal satisfaction a talented accessory designer receives from creating precious articles often outweighs the limited financial rewards for novices. The potential to earn in the millions for unique, sought-after creations is also an incentive to pursue this varied career field. Many accessory designers are self-employed, so salaries fluctuate greatly. On a general scale, based on recent government-compiled figures, average annual earnings of experienced full-time designers are nearly $56,000. The field is projected to grow more slowly than the average for all employment through 2014, but competition for jobs will remain keen because of the high level of interest in this industry.

The median salary for jewelers in retail stores is $27,400 annually. Most start with a base salary and then begin to earn more based on the number of pieces they complete. Those in sales may earn commissions in addition to their salaries. Most jewelers receive a variety of fringe benefits, including reimbursement from their employers for work-related courses and discounts on jewelry purchases.

The number of people employed as jewelers is expected to change little through 2014. However, employment opportunities should be good because of the number of jewelers who are retiring and the strong demand for jewelry. It's important to remember, however, that jewelry sales fluctuate, and downturns in the economy can have significant impact on the industry as a whole.

Jewelry sales are being fueled by an increasing number of affluent individuals, working women, and double-income families, as well as by the growing number of fashion-conscious men. Those older than forty-five also tend to account for a large percentage of jewelry sales, and that segment of the population is on the rise.

Earnings for shoe and leather workers vary greatly depending upon place of employment. To date, the job outlook for this occupation is expected to decline through the year 2014 as a result of growing imports of less expensive shoes and leather goods.

Some specialized fields offer more opportunity. The prospects for workers employed in the manufacture and modification of custom-made molded or orthopedic shoes are better than those for most other leather workers. This is a result of substantial expected growth in the senior population and an increasing emphasis on preventive foot care.

Nevertheless, accessory designers in all areas have ample opportunity for self-employment. For example, about 40 percent of all jewelers are self-employed. Many operate their own stores or repair shops, and some specialize in designing custom jewelry.

CHAPTER FOUR

Breaking into the Performing Arts and Specialty Apparel Worlds

It's hard to imagine *Dreamgirls* without the glittery costumes or a bride in an ordinary dress. In fact, life would be pretty boring without sharp minds whipping up specialty creations. While the obvious choice of most fashion designers is to create standard day or evening wear, a large sector opts to work in the performing arts and specialty apparel realms. Costume design is a fascinating field involving knowledge of theater arts. Other target markets include fashions for dancers and exercise enthusiasts, professional athletes, weddings and other special occasions, and uniforms for occupations or schools that require them. Another oft-neglected career choice is that of the professional dresser in the theatrical world.

In the entertainment industry, you might find employment as a resident designer for a theater, opera, or dance company. Some costume artists are also freelancers who work on special commissions. Besides knowing how to sketch designs, select fabrics, cut patterns, and sew, you will need to know how a director thinks and the mood he or she is trying to convey in a performance. Historical knowledge of costumes is crucial, as well as understanding how costumes interact with stage sets and how to produce garments that are easy to get in and out of during quick changes.

Other specialty designers, who work either independently or for larger manufacturing firms, require the same amount of knowledge and experience as general clothing designers. There is also an important customized aspect to the work that sets specialty designers apart. They typically must be familiar with the nature of the specialization and particular body types.

Hours vary depending on the demands of your clients but tend to be long. A lot of fashion designers would agree that they spend twenty-four hours a day thinking of new ideas for their creations. The same applies to costume and specialty apparel designers.

Professional dressers tend to have a variety of skills. Most professional dressers are seamsters who have a keen knowledge of the theatrical profession. They understand the details of theater, including timing, scene breaks, and the mood swings of temperamental stars whom they help get quickly in and out of costumes.

Costume Designers

As a costume designer, you must keep in mind that you will work with unusual fabrics and styles—many of which mirror the period of the production at hand. Therefore, in-depth research into the cuts, patterns, and materials used throughout history is mandatory. Also remember that you are designing clothes that must be seen from a great distance by an audience. Construct your garments on a large scale and learn how to work with durable thread that will lessen the wear and tear on these costumes.

If you are attracted to dramatic theater, opera, music, or dance from a behind-the-scenes perspective and you are a talented artist, then a career in costume design could be very rewarding. You will most likely work in a spacious studio, where you sketch ideas before cutting out a pattern. You will then spend time searching for rare combinations of fabrics at garage sales, flea markets, or thrift shops. The rest of your time will include costume fittings with performers, sewing, and making alterations. In addition, you will spend long hours in rehearsal.

Dancewear and Workout-Wear Designers

The worlds of dance and exercise go hand in hand. There is a great deal of crossover, with designers involved in specialized garments that are comfortable and allow their wearers sufficient muscle warmth and sweat absorption. When it comes to shoes, acute knowledge of the feet, types of dance exercises, and proper bone and tendon placement is necessary. Some craftspeople only make ballet slippers (an especially complex art form passed on from generation to generation), jazz boots, tap and character shoes, and running shoes. Some of the largest dancewear and exercise-wear outlets are Capezio, Leo's, and Freed of London. You may work as a designer for these firms or for smaller specialty stores. If you have the drive and additional entrepreneurial skill, you might open your own business.

For exercise enthusiasts, cotton and Lycra blends in shorts and halter tops are often bestsellers, mainly because the cotton allows the skin to breathe and better absorbs perspiration than does 100 percent Lycra. Women marathon runners frequently request jogger-style bras that provide extra support. Most exercise fashions are sleeveless to allow for greater freedom of movement. Lycra and spandex are important materials for supporting the veins in the legs.

Shoes, which serve to support the foot, are critical to a proper fitness regimen. Experts say that some of the best footwear features include a narrowing at the back of the heel inside the shoe that hugs the ankle and prevents the foot from twisting, a built-in high arch, a lot of airholes, cushioned soles, absorbency, and all-leather construction for added comfort.

These are just some of the points to keep in mind when pursuing a design career in dance and workout wear. Firsthand experience with dance or athletics may also give you important insights into the kinds of products that would be well received in this field. Although these garments have a utilitarian purpose, those who design them still require a strong sense of fashion in order to create products that are stylish as well as useful.

Designing for the Professional Athlete

If you are in the business of designing clothes for sports professionals and enthusiasts, you need to know about more than just fashion. You need to know a lot about the sport at hand, whether it is baseball, football, tennis, cycling, or figure skating. Beyond team uniforms, you will create a variety of warm-up and practice gear that is comfortable and healthy for an athlete's body. You also must have a keen understanding of human anatomy.

Because large outlet stores and manufacturers have cornered this market, you would most likely be employed in this type of environment, as opposed to being self-employed. If you have a background in both sports and fashion, your knowledge and expertise will be invaluable. Because you will meet with coaches and players, you have to speak the language and understand what kinds of products are durable and muscle friendly.

A whole special segment exists for the outdoor sportsperson (skier, hiker, mountain climber, hunter, and kayaker, for example), with new developments constantly in the works. The bulk of outdoor merchandise consists of jackets with breathable, water-repellent fabric on the outside and down or high-performance synthetic fillers (such as Thinsulate) on the inside for warmth. For example, a company called the North Face has developed durable clothing known as Tekware. Made from a new generation of synthetic and synthetic-cotton blend fabrics, it is reported to be comfortable to wear, rugged, abrasion resistant, and designed to wick away sweat and dry quickly.

Successful designers in this area understand that style and function are equally important. No matter which sporting activity, or activities, you choose, remember that these products must do more than make athletes look good. They also protect athletes from the perils of their activities.

Special-Occasion Apparel Designers

Bridal wear is probably the first type of special-occasion garment that comes to mind, and rightfully so, because the wedding industry is one of the largest and most popular in the fashion world. Other areas include attire for religious events and personnel, along with graduation gowns. The latter two fields are similar to sportswear, in that a big outlet or manufacturing firm handles these bulk orders and works with staff designers who turn their ideas over to the sewing department.

Bridal gown designers—who may also create veils and other accessories—have a number of career options. They can design their own custom lines, work at a specialty bridal boutique, or work in the bridal department of a large clothing store. Just as styles change for womenswear, they also go though different phases in the bridal arena. Keep in touch with these trends while putting your own personal stamp on your work. After all, most brides want something that represents their unique personalities.

A whole new language exists for this fashion segment, and designers must be attuned to it. For example, being able to distinguish between a portrait collar and an illusion front—or identify a Queen Anne neckline or leg-of-mutton sleeve—is an important skill. Satin, silk, and hand-beaded lace are among the delicate fabrics that are transformed into what you hope will be a sensational, eye-catching wedding ensemble.

Uniform Designers

Several occupations still require clearly recognizable uniforms. A few examples are medical personnel, law enforcement employees, military professionals, mail carriers, express delivery drivers, and students at private schools. As a uniform designer, your work may get somewhat monotonous because there is not a lot of room for creativity. Yet you will have plenty to do involving variations on traditional designs and meticulous detailing work.

Once again, you will most likely be employed at a large manufacturing firm that turns these products out in massive quantities. If you choose to specialize in uniforms, you will work in an atmosphere more akin to an apparel plant as opposed to a chic studio, where you create smashing designs that are displayed in blockbuster fashion shows. The work, however, is steady. There remains a need for uniform designers as long as a great number of high-profile professions require uniforms.

Professional Theatrical Dressers

For an in-depth look at the little-known profession of theatrical dressers, rent the 1983 film *The Dresser*, starring Albert Finney and Tom Courtenay. It details the backstage work of these unsung heroes. Theatrical dressers not only help performers get in and out of their costumes at rapid-fire speed, but they also wash and repair these costumes and have mastered the intricate mechanics of working with archaic clothing, including tightly laced corsets, spats, and enormous hoop skirts.

There is more to this unusual profession than simply helping actors with costume changes and alterations. You must never succumb to panic and always be resourceful. After all, on average, a quick change can last anywhere from twenty seconds to two minutes—and timing is everything. You also have to deal with long, erratic show-business schedules. One of the oldest unions and advocacy groups for theatrical dressers is the Theatrical Wardrobe Union Local 764, which has represented wardrobe personnel in New York since it was founded in 1919.

Because you will be dressing both unknown supporting actors and famous celebrities, be prepared to deal with any personality type. Actors depend on their dressers and sometimes form close relationships with them. At times, you may even be sought out for advice or act as a surrogate parent to the complex artists who make up the eclectic theatrical profession.

Getting Started

We'll explore the various ways to enter these career fields.

Costume Designers

One of the best places to test your costume design talents is in high school or with your local community theater group. Both give you the opportunity to create the look of small-scale shows and will familiarize you with the general workings of the theatrical world. Take basic sewing and design courses to sharpen your hand-stitching and pattern-cutting skills. Practice sketching, which is another vital aspect of this profession. Then spend time researching period fabrics, designs, and construction techniques. It also wouldn't hurt to take an acting or set design course to learn how to work within other disciplines of the theater.

In addition, you can prepare by seeing a lot of live shows and films for a basic understanding of trends, techniques, and types of costumes needed. In your spare time, visit costume shops and clothing boutiques to see how these specialized items are constructed. Tour museums, read books on costume design, and view movies with period costumes to develop an eye for various styles and time periods.

One clever way to get started is by auditioning as an extra, or supernumerary, in local theatrical or opera productions. This simply means standing in the background as a "living prop." This way, you gain firsthand experience wearing a costume that some-day you might want to design. You will also be able to see how the designs fit within the context of the production in progress and get a clear idea of some of the fabrics and detailing needed.

Specialty Apparel Designers

Whether you design bridal gowns, uniforms, or sports clothes, you will need the basic skills of a fashion designer. Sketching, cut-ting out patterns, selecting fabrics, and sewing are all part of the process. The only difference is that you are in a very specific niche market that has its own rules, guidelines, and procedures. And for any specialization, you must know your product inside and out.

If you enjoy skiing, for example, and are pursuing a fashion design career, pay attention to the gear you wear. Better yet, think of even more comfortable or lightweight ways of making this par-ticular product more appealing and practical. The same applies to other niches, such as dance or workout attire.

The bridal sector is very close to what high-fashion designers do. One major difference is that you are designing a very special garment that carries a lot of symbolism and sentiment with it. Your fabrics are exceptional and expensive, and intricate beading techniques are a major requirement for this field.

In other areas, such as uniforms and graduation gowns, you will be part of the mass-produced garment industry, joining forces with seamsters and tailors to do standard but high-quality work. Textile and art-related courses are a must. Experience working in garment stores or limited merchandise boutiques can also prepare you for your future.

Theatrical Dressers

First and foremost, to prepare for a career in theatrical dressing you must learn to become a top-notch seamster or tailor. That's the basis of your job. Enhance that by being able to do on-the-spot alterations or restyling. Like a typing student, time yourself to see how quickly you can repair, button, and lace hard-to-handle fabrics such as velvet and burlap. Then get out to the theater and watch as many shows as you can afford. One way to see a lot of shows free is by volunteering as an usher. Talk with backstage dressers—even ask to work as an apprentice.

As in costume design, you can gain experience by working with your school or community theater productions. In these venues, mistakes are just part of the learning process. That way, by the time you get to larger theaters, you will have mastered the split-second timing needed to move the show along flawlessly. Because choreography is crucial to the smooth running of any production, you must learn how to pace yourself and arrange your costumes in sync with the performance as a whole.

Education and Training

Find out how to improve your skills and prepare for your future career.

Costume and Specialty Apparel Designers

Educational options in costume design are many and varied. Some designers opt to work on the theater faculty of major universities, where they create costumes for local productions. Apprenticeships with area performing troupes are also quite popular. Apart from taking classes in acting, stagecraft, lighting, and scene and prop construction, your education would be very similar to that of general fashion designers. The same holds true for specialty apparel designers, who work in the clothing industry but attain more specialized knowledge through practical experience and understanding of a particular area.

The National Association of Schools of Art and Design has accredited approximately 250 institutions with programs in art and design. Most of these schools award a degree in art. Many schools do not allow formal entry into a bachelor's degree program until a student has successfully finished a year of basic art and design courses. Applicants may be required to submit sketches and other examples of their artistic ability.

Two- and four-year degree programs in fine arts exist throughout the United States and Canada, as well as two- and three-year professional schools that award certificates or associate's degrees in design. Graduates of two-year programs generally qualify as assistants to designers. An ideal liberal arts curriculum would include courses in art history, drawing, life (anatomical) drawing, garment construction, draping, pattern making, textiles, and merchandising. A few schools offer one-year programs in practical design. Studies stress applied skills rather than liberal arts courses.

Costume and specialty apparel designers should be computer literate. Computer-aided design skills are an important asset, especially for those who work for large manufacturers. Designers also use computers to research clothing styles and to market their creations.

Theatrical Dressers

No degrees are required to be a successful theatrical dresser. Experience is more important. The essential skills can be acquired through an apprenticeship with an established dresser, practice, and textile courses or workshops.

If you can't break into a theater immediately, apply for a job at a garment-manufacturing firm, where you can hone the tools of your trade. Even work at a dry cleaner can provide you with the experience needed to do all kinds of repairs and alterations. It will also familiarize you with the endless varieties of fabrics.

Finally, rely on your own confidence and talent to get to know actors, directors, and other theatrical dressers. Frequent restaurants or neighborhoods where the artistic community hangs out, and keep up with the top theater companies in your area as well as blockbuster touring shows. Don't be shy; networking will be key to your success.

Where the Jobs Are

Take a look at the range of potential employers in these fields.

Costume and Specialty Apparel Designers

Obviously, jobs for costume designers are in theater, dance, opera, and film. But there is also a small niche market of unusual costume shops and larger, more mainstream holiday-themed stores. You might want to explore the latter options before moving into stage work. Get your foot in the door early if you aim to become the next Edith Head, the world-renowned costume designer who won a slew of Oscars for her sensational work in Hollywood over the decades.

If you wish to pursue specialty apparel, learn as much as you can about these types of garments. Attend industry trade shows, such as bridal expos and uniform conventions. Look for a position as a seamster or designer assistant in a specialty firm or at a bridal store; then work your way up to a designer position.

Theatrical Dressers

Of course, the only option for theatrical dressers is to work backstage or on a movie set. Variations on the theme include special promotions outside theaters that require costume changes, or fund-raisers at hotels, for example, that include live entertainment. Fashion shows, too, require dressers.

Because theatrical dressers work in such a small, tight-knit profession, the craft is often passed on from generation to generation in families, or from mentor to student, and so on. This is one way of ensuring an ongoing, quality line of succession. But if you have the skills and decide to pursue this field, humble yourself—even volunteer—for backstage work until you get your big break. Think of yourself as taking a career route not much different from that of aspiring stars.

Opportunities and Earnings

Here's a sampling of salary projections in these career areas.

Costume and Specialty Apparel Designers

Because costume designers are more specialized than fashion designers, they don't have as many career opportunities open to them. If a ballet, opera, or theatrical company employs them, they would start at an annual salary in the mid to high teens, with the possibility of advancing to the high thirties or forties. It is difficult to give a general pay scale because costume design work is often sporadic and seasonal. Some of the best rewards are intangible, focusing more on artistic achievement and recognition than on high pay and bonuses.

There are also the few legendary exceptions to the rule. Big-time costume designers whose work is exceptional can earn profits in the millions. However, most costume designers will tell you that their incomes are modest, but their jobs are fun and fulfilling.

As in general clothing design, the average earnings for experienced full-time specialty apparel designers are $55,840 per year—slightly less for entry-level apparel firms. Design assistant positions pay about $500 a week. Designers at top companies can earn from $60,000 to $100,000 a year. They may become partners in the firm for which they design garments or start their own specialty companies.

Both arenas are competitive, and the supply typically outpaces the demand. Nevertheless, opportunities are available for the most talented and determined designers. It's up to you to find them. Employment in fashion design across the board is expected to grow more slowly than the average for all employment through the year 2014, and competition will remain keen.

Theatrical Dressers

The job outlook for this close-knit profession is not particularly bright. Theatrical dressers are not in great, constant demand, and the pay is often minimum wage or slightly higher. Yet it is an exciting profession, with opportunities for growth and satisfaction. If you enjoy the nomadic life, you might want to aim for a job as a full-time dresser for a touring troupe or act.

Like seamsters and tailors, most theatrical dressers earn between $351 and $443 per week. You can also supplement your income by doing alterations at a dry cleaner or clothing store. Some unions within the theatrical world provide health and insurance benefits to their members.

CHAPTER FIVE

Exploring Wholesale and Retail Careers

For all its glamour and prestige, the fashion arena would come to a standstill without assertive sales representatives and publicists getting the goods out to the public. And those individuals must be as competitive as the designers. Divided into wholesale and retail, this area is made up of movers and shakers who buy, sell, display, and promote the items created by designers.

When collections are ready to be unveiled, these important businesspeople are there following buying trends and making key decisions that will effectively set styles for their clients and the consumer public. Travel is frequent in the wholesale realm, and on-site work is more common on the retail side. Because of the long hours, competitiveness, and stress involved, a large percentage of fashion businesspeople suffer burnout, making job turnover quite common.

Don't be frightened off by the fast-paced, type-A aggression described here. The business end of fashion can be highly rewarding financially if you work hard and know how to pace yourself. You get to meet a lot of exciting—and eccentric—people, and your job is never dull.

To succeed, you have to be willing to put in long hours and demonstrate outstanding communication skills. Knowledge of business and fashion products is essential. Hone your skills and study fashion trends to remain several steps ahead of the competition, and don't take rejection personally.

You don't need a degree to be successful. However, education is always an advantage. It will enhance your natural talents as an outgoing person with a knack for talking confidently and enthusiastically about the items you are promoting.

Buyers and Sales Representatives

If you opt to become a buyer or sales representative, you will really be on fashion's cutting edge. A key decision maker in determining what styles will be most popular for a season, you will shoulder a lot of responsibility. It's important that you have a solid knowledge of fabrics, buying patterns, and fashion trends, along with some general business savvy, such as an understanding of pricing structures and bulk discounting.

Buyers and sales representatives work closely together. Sales reps spend a great deal of time calling or meeting with buyers to show the garments or accessories of the designer or firm they represent. If the buyer believes certain items will sell, he or she places an order.

Most major designers and design companies have their own permanent showrooms, where buyers view and purchase new collections. New York is the showroom capital of the world. Buyers go there many times a year for fashion week, the time when new collections are presented and sales made. Other fashion showroom sectors include Toronto, Dallas, Atlanta, Miami, Los Angeles, and Chicago, as well as Paris, Rome, and Milan for the international fashion scene.

A large percentage of sales reps work primarily in showrooms. Others work independently, contacting buyers before visiting them with a bundle of samples. Known as road reps, they spend substantial time on the road covering specific regions for their clients.

Buyers and sales reps who work out of designer showrooms are busiest just before and during fashion weeks—four to six times during the year when the seasonal fashion shows are held. Those employed by major manufacturers have more sanely paced schedules, but don't expect a standard nine-to-five workday. Sales reps typically arrange their schedules to suit buyers, and entertaining prospective customers often requires you to work well into the evening and on weekends.

Fashion Trade Show and Event Organizers

Designers rely on assertive trade show and event organizers to help market their creations to a large, concentrated segment of the industry. Trade shows are especially useful for jewelry and fabric designers. They are often organized through and held at major apparel centers around the world. As a trade show or event organizer, you work well in advance of targeted shows and are responsible for promoting the event to prospective exhibitors, selecting the exhibitors, and earmarking key individuals and companies to be invited to attend.

As a corporate executive, you will work nine-to-five days. But, because this is the unpredictable world of fashion, you would most likely put in several hours beyond that, as well as work some weekends.

A booming trade show area is the wedding apparel niche. Specialized bridal expos draw in some of the largest business and consumer crowds. Huge numbers of people gather for these events, which are held at large convention halls during prime season—fall shows featuring summer attire, for example.

The crème de la crème of the industry are the lavish and outlandish fashion shows that take place in elaborate tents erected on vast fairgrounds in New York, Paris, and Milan for the spring/summer and fall/winter collections. Some have called these events circuses, but that goes with the inherently show-business nature of fashion. The shows attract top celebrities, supermodels, and swarms of fashion journalists and photographers.

Organization of these shows is an ongoing process, with planners dealing with the capricious temperaments of famous designers and the mega egos and mood swings of big-name models. Nerves of steel and a resilient personality are absolutely necessary. This is definitely not an occupation for the faint of heart or easily intimidated.

Boutique Owners

The bottom line of any industry is making a profit. Once clothing and accessories are designed and manufactured, they reach the consumer market through stores. Big apparel chains and retail outlets make up a large segment of the market. However, if you prefer personalized service and unique designs, you will garner both personal and financial rewards by owning your own boutique or specialty store.

Although many fashion designers sell their products to department stores, many own their own boutiques. Even if you are not a designer, you can help designers by understanding that side of the business and promoting designers' work in your own store. As a retailer and business owner, your job requires a major time commitment, including work on weekends. Owning a business also requires accounting and marketing skills that are just as important as being familiar with the fabrics and styles a designer creates.

Fashion Window and Countertop Display Artists

If you consider yourself an artist first and a retailer second, working as a fashion window and countertop display artist could be an ideal career for you. This field is often taken for granted. How many times do you window-shop without thinking about the planning and artistry that go into this visual advertisement? How often do you breeze past fancy display counters, unaware of the creativity involved in making a store aesthetically pleasing? Probably quite often. Yet, the effect of eye-catching store exhibits is an important part of the selling process.

Called visual merchandising artists, managers, or directors, these insightful creators typically have backgrounds in art, theater design, or art history. They get their fashion experience on the job. Often they work their way up, decorating various departments in large stores.

Visual merchandising artists are part of a team. They work with store managers and other designers to invent a clever look that represents the store's philosophy. Then they tie that in with seasonal themes, humor, or citywide promotions, such as a summer festival, major sporting or theater event, or celebrity extravaganza.

Fashion Publicists

When designers and stores want to get the word out about their products to millions of prospective buyers, they work with a publicist—also called a promotional specialist or public relations representative. Fashion publicists are responsible for channeling the most crucial information about their clients to the media. Public relations is invaluable to this highly competitive industry; it includes working hand in hand with organizers of fashion shows, corporate-sponsored events, and national promotions.

Publicists can be self-employed, work for an agency, or be on the staff of a prominent fashion designer or retailer. They work around the clock in a corporate environment that makes relentless demands on their time and endurance. Most special events take place in the evening and on weekends. You must have a dynamic, enthusiastic personality—and be able to convince the media that the person or product you represent is the best. Publicists must sell constantly, always be on, and never get discouraged by the media's abrupt, curt manner.

Getting Started

Take a look at the following tips on how to begin your job search.

Buyers and Sales Representatives

Working part-time as a salesperson at a boutique or department store provides essential hands-on experience in the fashion business world. It also gives you a chance to track consumer buying habits and, in turn, get a head start on honing your own buying and selling techniques. Business courses help, too.

As a sales rep, your ability to initiate conversations over the telephone and in person, and to deliver an effective sales pitch, is mandatory. Start practicing early by volunteering for school or community fund-raisers. Or seek out sales jobs that require you to make cold calls. Then, if fashion is your calling, take general courses in textiles and fabrics. Read a lot of fashion magazines to learn the lingo, and keep a record of style trends and what influences them.

Fashion Trade Show and Event Organizers

If you are great at throwing parties, you will fit right into the frenetically paced world of organizing fashion trade exhibitions and special events such as groundbreaking fashion shows. However, you have to be extremely organized and driven to keep up in an arena where yesterday's "it" ideas are old hat today. Seasoned industry veterans are accustomed to attending so many specialized industry shows that their budgets force them to streamline by attending only the ones that will benefit them the most: the best-run, best-organized, and best-attended events.

It is your job to understand what the hottest product trends are and be able to discern what gets prospective customers excited. At school, you can get your feet wet by serving on the prom committee or by coordinating student fashion shows on a small scale. If you work in a store, volunteer to assist with promotions. Arts and crafts fairs are another venue where you can talk with organizers to get a feel for what they do.

Boutique Owners

One of the best ways to get into the retail business is by working in it. No special degrees are required, although courses in fashion design and accounting would help immensely. Success depends on your natural talent for working with people and determining which products will sell and which ones will fall flat.

Start by working as a sales clerk at a clothing store in your neighborhood. Talk to other boutique owners and find out how they made a successful leap to self-employment. Begin saving your money because, as a business owner, you will need capital to rent a space and purchase your merchandise.

Research neighborhoods that attract the type of business you wish to open—or find areas where you can break new ground. Work in various aspects of a store to discover how many hats you need to wear as a business owner—including obtaining necessary permits, doing accounting and inventory, buying items you plan to sell, and decorating the store.

Fashion Window and Countertop Display Artists

Early experience for visual merchandising artists may be as simple as helping your school librarian create special book exhibits or designing props for a local play. As long as you have an artist's talent and eye for appealing displays, you can pursue this field with confidence. The best training, however, is hands-on in a retail outlet, where you can assist store managers with seasonal window and in-store decorations.

You don't necessarily have to start out on the clothing floor. Most department stores place visual artists in various areas—from housewares to stationery. The key rests in your ability to draw attention to the products at hand.

Once you have moved up to the clothing or accessories sector, more on-the-job knowledge will ensue. This is a hands-on field in which you can really only learn by doing. Then your talent for matching textures, patterns, and cuts will begin to emerge.

Fashion Publicists

Because the fashion public relations field requires strong written and verbal communication skills, hone your craft by writing and submitting articles to your school newspaper and concentrate on public speaking. The debate club is an excellent means of practicing sales techniques, which a good publicist must have in order to get the word out on his or her client's business.

Publicists are very active in the organization of events, such as fashion shows. Therefore, you can gain valuable experience if you volunteer to assist with coordinating local festivities. A variety of opportunities exist, from a holiday reception to a student social to a writer's workshop.

There are many ways you can stay on top of trends and publicity options. Read all types of magazines and journals, especially to better understand what editors are drawn to. The Internet—with its online publications, blogs, and downloadable fashion sites—makes your research quicker and easier. And don't underestimate the value of watching TV to spot fresh opportunities to showcase a potential client.

Education and Training

Take a look at various opportunities for getting the education and training you need.

Buyers and Sales Representatives

Experience is probably the best education for individuals pursuing the buying and selling aspects of fashion. However, a certificate or a two-year or four-year degree in fashion merchandising or marketing and communication, paired with a minor in textile or fashion design, would be a strategically wise career move. With scores of aggressive businesspeople lining up to be part of the constantly changing fashion universe, it would work in your favor to have a degree to back up your qualifications, even if you are capable of selling bikinis to those fur-clad folks on the arctic tundra.

Computer skills are necessary in the high-tech business world. Advanced computer skills will allow you to research, market, and keep business records more effectively.

Fashion Trade Show and Event Organizers

A two-year or four-year degree in marketing and/or communication, combined with fine arts courses or a minor in textile or fashion design, will move your career in special events planning forward. Your academic experience will also help you perfect the necessary skills for survival in this hot-and-cold business. Marketing and public speaking courses will give you the know-how and confidence to accomplish the challenging and hectic tasks that await you on the job. Because fashion shows are a lot like theater, taking directing courses and working part-time backstage with a community or professional acting troupe could certainly boost your know-how and credibility.

With a basic understanding of textiles and fashion design terminology, you will be several steps ahead of other prospective event organizers who are not up on the fashion industry's language or structure. Being able to converse confidently and authoritatively will help you score points with your equally competitive superiors—paving the way for pay increases and job promotions within the profession's larger and more influential frameworks, such as New York fashion shows and big-name designer promotional blitzes.

Boutique Owners

Because most boutique owners are also designers, a degree in fashion design will certainly give you a solid foundation for producing quality garments. Those entrepreneurs who sell clothes for other designers should come to the floor equipped with at least general accounting and business courses, as well as an acute understanding of fabrics, cuts, and trends.

The most common progression for boutique owners involves starting out as a salesperson at a specialty or department store, then moving up to various buying and managerial levels before branching out on their own once they have done all the necessary networking and made solid industry contacts.

Fashion Window and Countertop Display Artists

Two- or four-year fine arts and design degree programs exist throughout the United States and Canada. Two- and three-year professional schools award certificates or associate's degrees in design. Visual artists in the retail realm frequently hold art degrees, with specializations in painting, sculpture, or photography. They are used to working with a variety of materials, which is a necessity for window and in-store displays.

Others find degrees in theater design and art history very useful because they learn how to build stage sets—which is what store exhibits are, essentially. These degrees also increase knowledge of artistic and historic themes and genres, which is useful when creating highly specialized displays.

Formal study, however, will only take you so far. It is important to find the right job because the rest of the preparation takes place in the workplace. Choose to work with someone whose skills you admire and would like to emulate.

Fashion Publicists

Most fashion publicists begin with a combination of formal study and real-world experience. A college education combined with public relations experience, usually achieved through an internship and work in the fashion sector, is considered excellent preparation for the career. Most students major in public relations, journalism, advertising, or communication.

Seen as a growing field, public relations is regarded as a major degree area at hundreds of colleges and graduate schools nationwide. Common courses cover public relations principles and techniques; management and administration, including organizational development; writing news releases, proposals, annual reports, scripts, and speeches; computer graphics; and research, emphasizing survey design and implementation.

Most colleges are affiliated with firms that provide on-the-job internships, for which students apply and go through an extensive interviewing process. Some pay a stipend as well as give college course credit, while others just provide the course credit and an impressive addition to your resume.

Where the Jobs Are

Learn about entry-level positions and advancement opportunities.

Buyers and Sales Representatives

In the personality-driven arena of fashion buying and selling, you can realistically get hired as a receptionist at a designer's showroom and work your way up to a managerial position. Nevertheless, a business degree can speed your advancement immensely. Buyers frequently get started in boutiques, then pursue contacts within a city's large apparel mart, where they hook up with influential companies that can utilize their expertise.

For sales reps who work in showrooms, the first step up the fashion rung is sales supervisor or assistant sales manager. In bigger companies, becoming a regional manager is an early sign of success. Sales reps even become presidents of manufacturing firms. Others form their own companies and represent various manufacturers.

Fashion Trade Show and Event Organizers

Many special events planners are initially employed in the public relations field, where such activities are part of their overall promotional duties. Business degrees and sales or marketing experience are common among fashion trade show and event organizers because their duties extend beyond publicity to actively selling their products to prospective exhibitors and clients.

Aspiring event planners often get involved in sporting events, citywide festivals, and fund-raisers, and they work within the travel and hospitality industries to get well-rounded experience. Once they have mastered their organizational skills, special events planners can move into specific professions, such as fashion, where they can apply a winning formula to a specialized industry.

Boutique Owners

If you have an entrepreneurial spirit combined with good fashion sense, owning a boutique could be fulfilling and lucrative. Freedom to purchase and sell designs you believe will turn heads is especially gratifying. If you are also a designer, you have created a built-in means for marketing your collections. Expect to master the money management skills needed to run a business, along with the stamina to work seven days a week.

Most important, don't jump into self-employment unless you have done extensive research—from location to customer buying habits. If you set your sights high, take at least three years to strategically plan this highly risky, but exciting, career move. Because you will most likely be transferring your skills from working in the retail clothing and accessories sector to your own business, you must continue to perfect the skills necessary for being a successful and profitable store owner.

Once you have scouted out a prime location, determine how much remodeling is needed and how the rent will affect your overall profit. Meet with designers whose collections are unique but marketable. If you start stocking too many outrageous items, your customers may end up browsing but not buying. Install the proper means of security, and get an up-to-date computer record-keeping system.

You may also want to work with a visual artist to create appealing window displays, along with a spacious, comfortable environment. Never stop scouring fashion's inner circles for trends and innovative style ideas.

Fashion Window and Countertop Display Artists

Many visual merchandising artists don't start out in the clothing business. Instead, they work as graphic artists, scene and prop designers, and even fine artists before discovering the world of retail. At that point, they may be assigned to create displays for other departments, such as housewares or sporting goods.

In the fashion arena, visual merchandising artists are masters at integrating social and historical themes with the visual appeal of garments and their endless textures. Experience in various sides of the retail business prepares these specialists for working with store managers and understanding the corporate chain of command. Although they have terrific ideas, visual managers are part of a team and must be able to take criticism and suggestions well and to integrate others' ideas into an aesthetically pleasing whole.

Fashion Publicists

New York is probably the best place to start as a fashion publicist because it remains the fashion capital of the world. The design industry may be tough to break into initially, so get experience by working at a public relations agency that serves fashion-related accounts. Or work as an account assistant in any field to perfect your writing and communication skills, then keep your eyes and ears open for job leads.

In this business, you have to move quickly. So, if designer Alber Elbaz is looking for an assistant to write advertising copy, go for it—even if the pay isn't that great—to get your foot in the door. Small opportunities can lead to big career moves.

A sensible place to apply would be the public relations departments of design schools or apparel centers. These areas could put you in touch with some of the top designers, retailers, and manufacturing firms. Large stores also have publicity departments, where you can get heavily involved in celebrity product promotions and grand openings.

Opportunities and Earnings

Earnings vary considerably and depend largely on your geographic location and the size of the employer.

Buyers and Sales Representatives

Salaries for buyers and sales representatives follow similar patterns, and the two occupations rely on each other. A buyer who works for a large firm is paid a salary with standard benefits provided by the employer. The average annual salary for wholesale and retail buyers is $42,230. Growth is expected to be slower than the average for all occupations through 2014.

Sales or road reps, who work independently, are paid exclusively on a commission basis, with an average commission rate of 6 to 10 percent of gross sales. This rate can get as high as 15 percent. Sales reps who work in showrooms receive a salary plus commissions. Because these reps enjoy the security of a weekly paycheck, their commissions are usually lower than those of road reps. In general, showroom reps earn an average annual salary of $45,400. Other perks include reimbursement for travel and car expenses and discounts on the company's merchandise. Employment is expected to grow about as fast as the average through 2014.

Although the majority of buyers and sales reps work in New York, sales reps can also look for employment in other major apparel centers, such as Toronto, Los Angeles, Dallas, Atlanta, and Chicago.

Fashion Trade Show and Event Organizers

Starting salaries are quite modest for newcomers to the event-planning industry. Beginners must put in a hefty number of hours and years before reaching salaries in the seventies or higher. If you are organizing a fashion show for top New York designers, and you have a viable track record, you can command fees of $100,000 or more—especially if you own your own event-planning company. Overall, however, salaries in managerial levels average in the low fifties. Opportunity for growth is outstanding in an industry that relies on such events to gain publicity and earn substantial profits. As in most areas of fashion, competition for jobs is intense. Beginners should prepare well and expect to pay their dues.

Boutique Owners

Because buying patterns shift radically depending on the economy, store owners encounter greatly fluctuating incomes. The first two years in business are typically the most difficult because huge chunks of capital are invested in getting the store up and running. Once a visible profit surfaces by the third year, entrepreneurs can expect to stay in business—provided they continue to keep up with trends, maintain quality, and price their garments attractively.

It is realistic to expect to begin with a zero profit and escalate to six figures over the course of a few years—depending on the economy. An ongoing pattern in business is self-employment. If you opt to have your own boutique, you won't be alone. To meet this demand, the government and associations within the fashion world have created various incentives, such as first-time business owner loans, for enterprising businesspeople.

Fashion Window and Countertop Display Artists

Employment in visual design occupations is expected to grow about as fast as the average for all occupations through the year 2014. Many openings will result from the need to replace those who leave the field. Growth in population and personal incomes is predicted to encourage increased demand for visual artists in the retail business. However, interest in this field is high, and competition for jobs is intense.

Visual designers generally have modest incomes. Merchandise displayers and window dressers have median annual earnings of $38,060.

Fashion Publicists

Median annual salaries of public relations specialists are $43,830. Corporate public relations specialists tend to earn more than those employed by public relations agencies. Some highly successful publicists earn salaries in the mid-seventies and higher.

Although the field is expected to grow faster than the average through 2014, competition among recent college graduates for public relations positions is expected to continue because it is a popular career choice and the number of applicants will most likely exceed the number of job openings. Degrees are essential, especially in the majors of communication, journalism, public relations, and advertising. People without the appropriate educational background or work experience will face the toughest obstacles in finding a public relations job.

Due to the downsizing of major corporations, including those in the fashion world, many public relations specialists are branching out on their own and contracting their services to top clients. Here the competition is fiercer than ever.

CHAPTER SIX

Working in Fashion Writing and Photography

Browse the Internet and the magazine racks of most bookstores and you will find that fashion publications are as popular as those devoted to sports and cooking. That's because the single most effective way designers get noticed is through the fashion media—from both an editorial and a visual perspective. Editors at top publications, such as *Vogue, Elle, Allure, GQ,* and *Women's Wear Daily,* wield so much power that design professionals constantly court them. These editors attend all the major seasonal fashion shows and determine what's hot and what's not. Even before the spring and fall collections are unveiled, these driven personalities meet with selected designers to get an idea of what's in store for future seasons.

Fashion writers and photographers have job options beyond the traditional fashion magazines. Fashion television and fashion websites and blogs are wildly popular. Other opportunities for writers involve penning the copy for store or mail-order catalogs.

In addition to the executive editors, the media world includes staff and freelance writers, managing editors, copywriters, production specialists, graphic artists, and photographers. Photographers work closely with editors, either through assignments or submission of their photos. Their careers run the gamut from photographing major fashion events for top publications to doing studio or on-location portraits of models to creating a prospective model's composites.

Fashion Journalists

Fashion journalists cover a wide range of topics, such as apparel, accessories, cosmetics, and fragrances. Today, all publishing activity is done on computers, so advanced computer skills—from layout to graphic design—are a must.

Journalists write under chronic deadline pressure in a competitive world, where hot stories and cool trends typically don't last out the month. Therefore, these sharp individuals must forever think of fresh story ideas and pursue angles that will hold the public's interest.

Most writers would agree that there is a highly charged feel to this massive industry. Fashion writers attend fashion shows around the world, interview famous designers and models, and report on colorful promotional events and new products. They don't have a typical nine-to-five office routine.

Editors plan their publications and assign stories to key reporters. They oversee production and edit articles as they come in. But, because they can make or break a designer, these editors also know their advantageous place in the fashion "food chain." They are often aloof, eccentric, and powerful people. Most have paid their dues as proofreaders, copywriters, and assistant editors.

An effective fashion editor is often someone who has worked extensively in the fashion business but also has a degree and experience in journalism. Fashion editors generally work in New York, Los Angeles, Toronto, and Montreal at well-established magazines or large-circulation daily newspapers, although there are a number of regional publications that can have just as high an impact on designers.

With the abundance of cable TV options and Internet access, fashion continues to be a profitable broadcast venture. Jobs are available in television production and scriptwriting for numerous style-related programs.

Catalog Copywriters

Employed either full-time for a company or on a freelance basis, copywriters produce advertising copy for use by store or mail-order catalogs to promote the sale of goods and services. Unlike journalists, copywriters have long lead times and don't experience such a hectic deadline crunch. Nor are they required to be aggressive or competitive. Copywriters are recruited for the ability to write sharp, concise prose that not only describes a garment or accessory but also prompts the consumer to buy it.

Copywriters work regular hours, with some flexibility, and they can also transfer their writing skills to advertising agencies that work with fashion-related accounts. Many writers are working in cyberspace, penning product descriptions for websites.

Fashion Photographers

Fashion photography is very similar to journalism, with most photographers sending their pictures to magazines and newspapers. Fashion photographers work in the same lightning-paced environment as journalists, often vying for the best vantage points at big, international fashion shows. They spend long hours setting up photo shoots and working with models in a studio or on location. Although some fashion photographers still develop their own film, high-end digital cameras have given many photographers a greater competitive edge, since long hours developing film are becoming a thing of the past.

The competitive nature of fashion photography usually drives photographers to perform better. They travel to glamorous places around the globe with professional models in tow. Fashion aficionados view their photos worldwide. But photographers in the world of high fashion are under constant pressure, especially when it comes to deadlines. Fashion photographers work odd hours and often maintain a brutally hectic pace. You really have to love the excitement and adventure to stick with this glitzy but harrowing profession.

Getting Started

There are usually a number of options for getting in the door. Here are some ideas to consider.

Fashion Journalists

One of the best places to start preparing for a career in fashion writing is online or at an area bookstore. Scan the vast array of fashion-related publications to get a feel for editorial style and content. Then subscribe to those magazines that most interest you, and continue to study them and learn key fashion phrases and buzzwords. Keep a file of some of the best-written articles.

In order to write proficiently about clothes and accessories, you need to know how they are made. Working at a boutique or department store will enhance your knowledge of the retail world. Join the staff of your school's newspaper or yearbook to get first-hand practice at reporting, working under deadline pressure and, most importantly, writing. Attend local fashion events and write articles to submit to local newspapers. This gives you an opportunity to practice applying your writing skills and may even result in a published "clip" to send to prospective editors.

Catalog Copywriters

As an aspiring catalog copywriter, your curriculum should reflect the same types of courses taken by aspiring fashion journalists. Add to your fashion magazine collection the countless catalogs and mail-order brochures posted your way. Study these in order to mold your writing into a concise, promotional style.

Familiarize yourself through research with the fashion industry. You do not, however, have to have a fashion design education. Being able to write effective copy is your most important asset. Therefore, work for your school's publications and seek part-time employment at a local newspaper. If you work in an office, practice writing correspondence, flyers, and other publicity-related materials in order to prepare for the highly specialized writing you plan to do.

If you enjoy both journalism and copywriting, pursue both by ultimately freelancing for publications and catalog companies. Promote yourself through your own fashion blog or podcast. Remember that freelance writers must spend years building a reputation through comprehensive portfolios that reflect numerous writing styles. Consistently and actively market yourself because, in this case, your pay matches the amount of copy you write. Unlike staff writers, a freelancer cannot rely on a steady paycheck. Yet the freedom and ability to earn large sums in the long run are very appealing incentives.

Fashion Photographers

The first thing you want to do if you intend to become a fashion photographer is buy a camera that you can carry around as often as possible. This way, if a terrific photo opportunity occurs, you will be ready to capture it. Although photographing models is a specialized industry niche, it is important for you to master the art and technique of photography before focusing on a specific subject.

Team up with an established photographer who can serve as your mentor, or work at a camera store or glamour-shot studio. Get accustomed to the myriad styles of cameras, lenses, attachments, and lighting equipment. Take a photography course or workshop, and subscribe to photo trade magazines. Join a photography club that would allow you to go on group photo excursions. Also take photos for your school's newspaper and yearbook.

Then, if fashion is your calling, collect some of the most stunning photographs from style publications and learn from them. If you can't find a photographer willing to teach you the trade at his or her studio, seek employment at an advertising or public relations agency that has fashion accounts. Or pursue employment at a large design firm, where you work exclusively with designers and the models they select to best show off their creations.

Education and Training

An academic background is important for most careers in fashion writing and photography.

Fashion Journalists and Catalog Copywriters

Although fashion is your focus, the journalism profession requires a liberal arts college degree in communication, journalism, or English. By also bringing to your resume experience in the retail or wholesale style fields, you increase your chances of breaking into the big league New York fashion publications. As a writer or editor, you must be able to express ideas clearly and logically. Mastery of electronic publishing, graphics, and video production equipment is also useful.

Because many editorial offices are arranged in cubicles, where phones ring often and other reporters conduct interviews surrounded by the sounds of office equipment, you must be able to concentrate amid confusion and produce under pressure.

Editors should display wise judgment in deciding what story ideas to accept and to reject. Like good writers, editors should understand their audiences. They should also display a balanced ability to guide and encourage others in their work.

A very popular, and effective, option available to college journalism students is the internship experience at magazines, newspapers, and broadcast stations. These programs run in conjunction with college courses and offer credit toward a degree, combined with very practical experience that can lead to a full-time job. Some internships also pay. You will work alongside experienced professionals who can guide you in writing short articles, doing research, and conducting interviews.

Because catalog copywriters follow similar paths as journalists, the educational requirements are basically the same, with emphasis on writing-based liberal arts courses. Art and textile courses are also useful. Computer literacy is a must.

Fashion Photographers

Many entry-level jobs in photography ask for little formal preparation. However, those in photojournalism generally require a college degree in photography or photojournalism. Employers seek applicants with technical understanding of the field and personal qualities such as imagination, creativity, and willingness to take risks. Completing an internship for a newspaper or magazine is an excellent way to gain experience and entry into this tight-knit field.

Commercial photographers must continually foster original ideas, and portrait photographers must have a natural knack for helping people relax in front of the camera. Photojournalists must understand the story behind an event so that their pictures match the story.

Many photographers choose to open their own studios, which adds a business dimension to their educational requirements. If you want to go it alone, you will need to know how to bid for and write contracts, hire and direct models, acquire permission to use photographs of people, price photos, and keep financial records. Some self-employed photographers try to enter the fashion world by submitting unsolicited photos to magazines with the long-term goal of contracting with them to shoot photos to accompany articles.

Where the Jobs Are

Where do you begin looking for a job?

Fashion Journalists and Catalog Copywriters

As discussed earlier, internships with magazines and newspapers are one of the most promising job-search tactics for fashion writers, providing much-needed experience while allowing for trial and error. Other techniques involve joining a journalism club that regularly invites professionals to speak at its functions. Get to know these professionals. Send them a resume and writing sample. Be persistent.

Before venturing into the ultracompetitive high-fashion publishing arena, get your start as a copywriter or assistant editor at a trade or consumer magazine. Meanwhile, network at fashion events—especially trade shows where publications sponsor booths—and collect editors' business cards. Learn when they are off deadline and call or e-mail to introduce yourself. Then send them information about yourself and follow it up with another call or e-mail. To avoid embarrassment, it's a good idea to find out editors' preferred modes of communication: e-mail, phone, or snail mail.

If you are determined enough, and happen to be an engaging writer, editors will most likely appreciate your moxie. On the other hand, if no one asks you to come in for an interview for a staff position, go out and get your own stories, which you can try selling, as a freelancer, to these same types of publications. That's another effective way of getting, if not your foot, at least your pen in the door.

Catalog copywriters should pursue similar, albeit less aggressive, routes by sending writing clips to advertising agencies that work with brochure and publicity writers. Through word of mouth and industry contacts, they can progress to the fashion industry, writing copy for department stores, specialty boutiques, and major manufacturers.

Fashion Photographers

Besides working alongside a photographer mentor or at a camera store, you can send out more job-search antennae by joining an active photography club or related organization. The National Press Photographers Association (NPPA) is dedicated to the advancement of photojournalism—a category that includes fashion shoots. Members include still and television photographers, editors, students, and representatives of businesses that serve the photojournalism industry. In addition to sponsoring educational events and workshops, NPPA offers members a job information bank.

As part of a professional organization, you will also get your name out and make contacts that will help you land a job. If fashion is where you want to be, make it a point to know which designers to approach and the most career-boosting parties to attend.

Opportunities and Earnings

What kind of paycheck should you expect?

Fashion Journalists and Catalog Copywriters

Salaries for fashion writers and catalog copywriters basically follow the scale for journalists in other areas of specialization. According to recent government figures, salaries for writers average $44,350 annually. Those at the highest level can earn more than $90,000. Editors earn an average of $43,890 a year, with those in the top 10 percent earning in excess of $80,000. Perks include paid travel expenses, discounts on clothes and other fashion items, and hefty room for growth.

Through the year 2014, the outlook for most writing and editing jobs is expected to remain competitive because of heavy interest in the field. Employment of salaried writers and editors is predicted to increase with the growing number of specialized and online publications. In fact, online publications are growing in number and sophistication, spurring the demand for writers and editors with Web experience. Due to the high cost of paper, many catalog companies are also transferring their products and descriptions to online information routes. Opportunities will also be created as current members of the profession retire or transfer to other occupations.

Fashion Photographers

The median annual salary for full-time salaried photographers was about $26,080 in 2004, with high earnings in the $50,000-a-year range. Many fashion photographers are self-employed, so their earnings fluctuate. Overall, they earn less than salaried employees, and their pay is affected by the number of hours they work, economic conditions, and their self-promotional abilities. Their biggest perks are travel and freedom to work outside the confines of an office.

Although employment of photographers is expected to grow at an average rate through the year 2014, aspiring shutterbugs outnumber the jobs available. Therefore, only the most skilled and those with the best business ability and willingness to adapt to rapidly changing technologies will be able to find salaried positions or attract enough work to support themselves as self-employed photographers.

If you plan to open your own studio, you should start saving now. Self-employed photographers incur considerable costs because of the need to purchase and maintain their own equipment and accessories.

CHAPTER SEVEN

Teaching in the Fashion World

You may be a fashion or accessory designer, but you get a great deal of satisfaction passing on your knowledge to the next generation. If that's the case, consider becoming a fashion instructor. With applicable degrees and a sufficient amount of industry experience—along with a natural ability to communicate your ideas before a diverse group of students—you can find a job teaching at a design school or in the textile department of a trade school, college, or university.

Depending on the number of classes you teach, you can create a flexible schedule that allows you time to research fabrics and keep up-to-date on materials and techniques while instructing a class and continuing to create and market your own fashions.

Other areas that fall under the fashion education category are style and makeup consultants, who advise, for instance, corporate clients on how to dress for success or conduct workshops at department store cosmetic counters. Another similar profession is that of clothing and makeup stylists, who set up fashion shoots for print media and television.

Textile and Design Instructors

The majority of textile and design instructors are based in colleges and universities. Overall, these faculty members teach and advise thousands of full-time and part-time students in the United States and Canada. In specialized fashion institutes, a large number of teachers work part-time and divide their days between lecturing and active demonstration. Therefore, your classroom is more like a workshop, where students sketch garments, cut out patterns, and sew. It's up to you to critique their creations, grade them, and give them constructive advice on improving their work and preparing for productive careers in fashion design.

If your specialization is draping fabrics or hat making (millinery), for example, it would be logical to teach those types of courses. As a designer, and possibly an owner of your own boutique, you can lecture on the business and marketing skills fashion entrepreneurs need for becoming self-employed. Supplement your classes by organizing field trips to apparel centers or textile museums.

As a fashion instructor, you will spend much time preparing your lectures and class assignments. If you also work as an independent designer, you will need to budget your workload so that you can devote complete attention to your various specialized tasks. Strong organizational skills and a willingness to put in long hours are a must.

Because design schools offer intensive, hands-on courses, be prepared to teach two long classes per day—one in the morning and one in the afternoon or evening. A design class typically lasts about three hours and involves a one-hour lecture accompanied by visual aids, with the remaining two hours devoted to sketching, cutting out patterns and material, and draping fabric on a dress form.

If your school day finishes around 4 P.M., you still have time to work on your own design projects into the evening. Outside classroom activities include advising students, grading, and assisting with the school's fashion shows.

Fashion and Makeup Consultants

Fashion and makeup consultation is a varied industry with many career options. Many clothing consultants—sometimes called personal shoppers or image management experts—come from the design and/or retailing sectors, where they have made, bought, or sold garments, which has taught them all they need to know about quality products and customer preferences. Consultants may have their own businesses with individual clients, ranging from society women planning their formal or travel wardrobes to corporate executives and political figures whose images depend upon their attire.

Other exciting arenas exist for fashion consultants. Some are on the staff of a department or specialty store, where they advise consumers on the custom attire they are purchasing. Others work in the theater and film worlds, where their special sense of color and texture blends are put to productive use. Makeup consultants also work in the show-business realm. More frequently, you will find them doing demonstrations at cosmetics counters or fashion events. They spend years blending products and inventing new looks—the result of education at a cosmetology institute paired with on-the-job experience and a lot of personal trial and error.

Clothing and Makeup Stylists

Like food stylists in advertising, clothing and makeup stylists work closely with a fashion photographer or camera operator in setting up fashion shoots for print media and television. They dress models and touch up makeup so that the lighting shows a client's products at their most appealing. With much experience working backstage at fashion shows or in the theater, these artistic personalities are responsible for helping determine attractive camera angles and performing a variety of duties that help make clothes and accessories look perfectly smashing.

Most of the qualifications for stylists are rooted in experience in fashion design, retail, wholesale, or even the modeling profession. This is a field that offers a plethora of opportunities. Success is based on an individual's talent, persistence, and willingness to work behind the scenes in an interesting mix of interrelated jobs.

Getting Started

Consider some of the following options for getting an early start on your career.

Textile and Design Instructors

A wise combination of courses for future textile and design instructors to take in high school are textiles, art, public speaking, and business. With this background, you begin your preparations for a well-rounded career in design and learn to feel comfortable speaking about various topics in front of a group. Volunteer as a tutor to determine if you have the ability to instill confidence in your students. You can even talk with your current teachers about conducting after-school workshops in whatever subject might be beneficial to you and your peers.

Research colleges that emphasize design and education. If your heart is set on fashion design, help organize a local fashion show or work part-time in retail. Sketch design ideas and make outfits that elicit praise from your friends, family, and mentors. Research to familiarize yourself with the latest advancements in apparel technology, such as digital sewing machines and adjustable dress forms, to develop a facility with equipment you will be using in the classroom.

Fashion and Makeup Consultants

Because fashion and makeup consultants enter their fields from so many different angles, just about any job or hobby that involves these subjects could pave the way for you. Besides getting involved with your school's fashion shows or theatrical productions, you should seriously consider working part-time at a boutique, department store, or cosmetics counter.

Keep a scrapbook of clips you have saved from fashion magazines to observe what types of clothing ensembles work together effectively. Spend a lot of time in stores, where you can feel fabrics and experiment with different color and texture combinations.

When it comes to makeup, get your friends involved. Ask them if you could try certain eye-contouring or lip-painting techniques on them. Experiment with makeup and hairstyle ideas on yourself, too. Then determine which field suits you best.

Clothing and Makeup Stylists

Observation is probably your best way to start. Try to understand compositionally what makes a photograph or movie scene stand out in your mind. Stylists are hired for their instinctive expertise at setting up a scene that is visually appealing. Experience and self-training are prudent routes to take.

You can also get experience by working in the fashion or photography arena as a sales representative or photography assistant. Experience in theater, especially within a costume department, will also prove invaluable. Knowing fabrics and how light plays with color are crucial, as is sharp vision.

Read as many fashion magazines and books as possible. Start a photo collection of ads and catalog shots that show styling at its most provocative and eye-catching. Working as an extra in a movie or with a local theatrical company can give you firsthand experience at observing behind-the-scene stylists in action.

Education and Training

Here are the skills and knowledge you need to pursue a successful teaching career in fashion.

Textile and Design Instructors

Teaching students about clothing and accessory design techniques, marketing skills, and the history of the business puts you in a hands-on, participatory realm. No matter where you're working—a high school, college, university, or design school—never underestimate your abilities as a significant faculty member. You may have to publish treatises or pass periodic oral examinations to be given tenure, which protects professors from being fired without just cause and due process. Usually, however, your expertise is expressed by the quality of fashion associations to which you belong, the latest collection you've just unveiled, or the number of fashion shows you organize.

In the fashion field, most faculty members are hired as instructors or part-time assistant professors. They typically hold a master's degree or doctorate in fine arts or textiles for employment at four-year institutions. A bachelor's degree plus experience in the field is generally sufficient for teaching in a two-year design college, although a master's degree is preferred.

Technology is changing the face of this segment of the fashion industry. More and more schools are dependent upon computerized sewing machines and pattern cutters, as well as electronic grading systems. To prepare your students for the marketplace, you will need to become adept at using the latest technology.

Because fashion education centers offer courses from fabric design to drawing and merchandising, you want to find an area where you excel. Then get experience in that particular sector, supplement your education with community activities or fashion seminars, and start a portfolio of your best work.

Hone your oral and written communication skills and get accustomed to establishing rapport with your students. Finally, be prepared to work in an environment where you receive little direct supervision.

Fashion and Makeup Consultants

The exciting part about becoming a fashion consultant is that you're not restricted to any particular segment of the industry. You could hold a bachelor's degree in public relations, work on major designer accounts, then branch out into your own consulting business. Or you may be a designer or boutique owner, with a fashion design and marketing background. These are just a sampling of the doors through which you can enter the fashion consulting business.

For makeup consultants, the road is more structured. They traditionally attend a two-year cosmetology program at an institute that specializes in hairstyling, makeup application, and manicures. These learning centers, which are more akin to trade schools than academic institutions, promote hands-on learning with apprenticeships. They are also excellent sources for employment and usually place graduates in a variety of beauty-related jobs. Ultimately, if you are an exceptional makeup artist, you can serve as a consultant for big-time movie studios, fashion designers, or lavish theatrical productions.

Clothing and Makeup Stylists

A fine arts background in fashion design, photography, or graphic art would be an excellent supplement to your career as a clothing or makeup stylist. On-the-job training is even more crucial than formal education. In fact, timing and a good eye for detail—teamed with an assertive disposition and willingness to work long, unpredictable hours—may be enough to land you a financially rewarding and personally fulfilling job.

As in most areas within the competitive fashion industry, experience is your best teacher. Since you will work primarily with photographers and camera operators, set your sights on finding a job in these types of studios. Study and teach yourself what styles blend well together, and visit clothing and accessory stores regularly.

Where the Jobs Are

Explore the following options for entry-level jobs.

Textile and Design Instructors

Once you have completed the necessary academic requirements and have some substantial experience under your belt, you are ready to land that first job in fashion education. One effective way is through substitute teaching. If you are a designer or fashion educator in the making, you could decide whether you are cut out for teaching at a fine arts or design school by filling in for an instructor who is on vacation.

You may even want to begin as a lecturer, gaining practice speaking at fashion association functions. Teach your own fashion workshop or seminar. Or get your name out as a designer first, then bring your expertise to the classroom.

The beautiful part about textile and design instruction is that you don't have to do it full-time. It can be a supplement to fostering your design career. Most importantly, it can fill your need to pass on your fashion education to aspiring designers.

Fashion and Makeup Consultants

Networking is the key to breaking into the consulting business because it is typically an independent form of employment, one in which your paycheck is only as dependable as your recently acquired account. If you start out in any aspect of the industry, whether it be fashion design, sales, or public relations, get to know the key movers and shakers who might be interested in hiring you as a consultant. Attend all the important trade events and fashion shows, and be a master of sophisticated self-promotion.

As a makeup consultant, look for job openings at department store cosmetic counters and fill out a variety of applications. If show business intrigues you, get your name out to talent agencies, who could refer models and photographers to you as well as let you know when someone is filming a movie in town. Networking in this realm is a top priority.

Clothing and Makeup Stylists

Photography studios, advertising and public relations firms, and talent agencies are excellent places to seek employment as a clothing or makeup stylist. This is the type of profession in which you could work your way up from apprentice or assistant positions to high-level style directors who have the final say on how a fashion ad or TV commercial is going to be seen by the public. But that depends on your motivation and consistent talent for creating successful visual ad campaigns.

This is not a good career choice for introverts. Networking is key to success. A tight-knit business, clothing and makeup styling allows its professionals to move around in fashion circles based on word of mouth and a solid, respected reputation.

Opportunities and Earnings

Check out what's out there and how much you can earn.

Textile and Design Instructors

Earnings for fashion instructors vary according to the types of schools that employ them and their levels of experience. Faculty in four-year institutions earn higher salaries, on the average, than those in two-year schools. According to recent government figures, salaries for postsecondary educators average $51,800.

Those figures drop slightly when applied to high schools and the fine arts profession, as opposed to higher education programs in science or business. A top perk is having summers off and long holiday breaks to attend to other fashion projects, especially if you are a designer. You also have access to top fashion companies and professionals through your affiliation with a design school.

Employment of college and university faculty is expected to increase faster than average for all occupations through 2014, with a significant number being part-time positions.

Fashion and Makeup Consultants

As in other aspects of fashion, salaries for fashion and makeup consultants are wide open, with higher earnings contingent upon how many prosperous accounts you land if you choose to work independently. You can begin earning as little as $20,000 a year, then escalate to salaries in the sixties. Corporate positions, as you might expect, are the highest paid.

Department store makeup consultation is lower paying, especially at the entry level. This is attributable to the fact that many makeup consultants are also sales clerks, who generally earn a salary in the high teens that is supplemented by a commission. There is room for advancement, with supervisory positions available. You can also team up with a fashion consultant and start a partnership.

Clothing and Makeup Stylists

Once again, there is no set salary for clothing and makeup stylists. Most stylists start at the bottom of the ladder, earning an hourly minimum wage, while proving themselves. If you get an early start and work with a mentor who really likes your work and introduces you to photographers and advertising executives, your success could skyrocket, and you can command much higher wages.

The option for doing freelance styling is also available. In this segment of the industry, you can negotiate hourly and annual wages and benefits.

With companies constantly searching for bigger and better ways to advertise, stylists are expected to remain in demand. Catalogs and ads are available on the Web, where literally billions of people can view them. Industry bigwigs, therefore, want to employ the best and brightest for their fashion ad campaigns—and stylists are crucial to conveying the company's attention-grabbing look.

CHAPTER EIGHT

Modeling Fashions

The steady rise of the supermodel—from icons Cindy Crawford and Naomi Campbell to more recent divas like Heidi Klum and Gisele Bündchen—has prompted countless young girls to expect to hit it big in the runway biz. High salaries, glamorous lifestyles, and the potential to date rock stars and other hot celebrities form a major part of modeling's appeal. But, alas, the perks can come at a cost. So if you have read up to this point and have a clear idea of fashion's tough realities, you might want to pay even closer attention to the honest advice we provide about the modeling industry.

Fashion modeling is a highly competitive realm. Because it is such a glamorous, high-paying field, fashion modeling has attracted opportunists who are often more interested in taking advantage of you than in advancing your career. Hence, there are two words of caution you should heed in this business: be careful.

We will discuss the necessary background information and job prerequisites, but the bulk of this chapter focuses on how to approach an overcrowded industry—inhabited by people our society has deemed, according to its standards, extremely beautiful—and survive within its highly judgmental confines.

Keep in mind that there are just a handful of supermodels like Oluchi Onweagba and Alessandra Ambrosio. Most successful models establish a local presence and get work modeling for clothing catalogs, special events, or runway shows. Others make a career of modeling for corporate training films, called industrials, and promotional videos. There is also a very small niche market that involves modeling only certain exceptionally attractive body parts, such as hands, legs, feet, and teeth, for print advertising and television commercials.

Runway, Print, and Film Models

Although one may initially think that all a model needs to succeed are great looks, poise, and perfect posture, this is a complex, far-reaching business that covers numerous subcategories. It's also an industry in constant flux. Depending on what the latest craze is, you could find that your curvaceous frame and pouty lips get you on the cover of most magazines for a year, only to be ignored the following year in favor of the latest rail-thin waif.

For this reason, it is important that you create as many options as possible. For example, if you are a woman at least five feet, seven inches tall and keep your weight at a healthy minimum, plus have a face that can acquire various looks with creative makeup applications, you might want to consider runway modeling. Men in this profession tend to be six feet tall or more, muscular, and display chiseled features. This career involves extensive training in how to walk and show any type of ensemble to its best advantage.

Not only will you travel frequently, but you will work long, odd hours that drastically reduce your social life. The irony here is that models, while extremely busy, must socialize in order to make important contacts. Parties remain one of the best networking arenas. In this flamboyant, eccentric business, you must, however, always be aware of the con artists and sweet-talking "agents."

If you are too short for runway modeling but have an alluring face and charm, then print advertising or television commercials are probably where you belong. Most models register with a reputable agency following basic training. It's your responsibility to follow up with these agencies to let them know you are interested and to keep up with all the important auditions—even if you're going on an audition for a laundry detergent commercial or the telephone company's latest training video.

Modeling, with its many facets, is a vital part of the fashion industry. Know that there are millions of people with your ambition and that only a few really make it big due to the right mix of talent, timing, connections, and good fortune. Don't get discouraged by the competition. Get motivated by it. Put your name and face out there to people who matter. Then capitalize on your unique attributes to set yourself apart from all the rest.

Although certain sectors exist for more mature models, modeling is primarily a career reserved for the young. So pursue it with vigor as early as possible. Most important, have a backup career in case you keep getting rejected or grow dissatisfied with the modeling profession and its persistent search for the perfect face or body.

Specialty Models

If you have been consistently told that you have perfect teeth, beautiful hands, or shapely legs, you should seriously consider becoming a part-time specialty model. Just flip through a magazine. How many ads do you see with just certain body parts displayed—a hand holding a fork, for example? Decidedly many.

Well, these are real-life models who are frequently sought out by companies that request specialized talent through agencies at which the model is registered. Unlike full-body modeling, this niche market tends to be very sporadic, with unpredictable opportunities. Even these opportunities require auditions, which means that you show up in person at a photography studio, and if you have the look a creative director is seeking to capture, you will be hired on the spot. Then you are paid on an hourly basis for the time it takes to create the print ad or television commercial.

For most, specialty modeling is not a full-time job. Because assignments are few and far between, it is a good idea to have a full-time job. Just look for one with a flexible schedule that allows you to respond to audition requests on short notice.

Getting Started

Here is some advice on taking those first steps toward a modeling career.

Runway, Print, and Film Models

Of course, some models get started as infants or children. But that doesn't necessarily guarantee success as adults. More commonly, models begin honing their skills in high school, doing part-time work for catalogs. Another way to practice is through participation in local fashion shows, as well as taking movement classes, signing up for a fashion workshop, and registering with a reputable modeling and etiquette school.

It is extremely important to do your research. Check with the Better Business Bureau or an accredited association that monitors talent-related operations. If you call an agency and are asked to come in for an audition, do not go unaccompanied. This applies to both men and women. It simply can't be stressed enough how many scams have been discovered within the modeling profession.

Ads promising high salaries, travel, and extensive exposure are the ones to watch out for and vigorously ignore. As determined as you may be to fulfill your fashion-modeling dream, don't make any hasty decisions. They could not only cost you money, but they could also harm you. So, now that we've cleared the air on that matter, we will talk about what to do first.

Contact a local talent agency, one that is well known and respected. Ask for the representative who handles print and film or runway models and make an appointment for a free consultation. Another word of caution: make sure that the consultation is free. If an "agent" asks you for money to help get you work, run the other way. Not only is this unlawful, it should tip you off to a scam in the making.

The agency representatives should be able to honestly evaluate your potential. They look for unusual, exaggerated features that border on exotic; fresh-faced girl-next-door appeal; dark, rugged masculine types; or any styles that would convey a designer's message. Ask the rep to supply you with the names and phone numbers of professional fashion photographers who can be trusted with creating your composites. Information on photographers can also be obtained from national photography associations.

In this industry, composites are your entrée into your career. Composites are a series of photos of you in four or five different poses and looks. Most commonly, composites are printed in color on high-quality paper, with information on your vital statistics (age, height, weight, and so on). Once you have done your research on photographers, set up an appointment for a full-day or half-day photo session.

After the shoot is completed, review proofs and select the ones you believe will catch the eye of a talent agent. Once your composites are ready (print about five hundred of them initially), call the best agencies in your city. Set up a time when you can register and bring in a stack of your composites. While you are at the agency, you will be required to stamp the agency's address on the back of your "comps," which they, in turn, mail to advertising agencies, designers, photographers, and so on. Agencies also post composites on their websites. If you have the look a client hopes to project, you will be called in for an audition that involves photographing you, for example, in fall fashions.

Once you are hired, you will work long, sometimes backbreaking hours getting fitted and modeling for the camera. If a runway assignment becomes available, be prepared to expend a lot of energy to make it through fittings, rehearsals, and the ultraquick changes during the actual fashion show. You will be paid hourly, with a commission going to the agency that books you.

Finally, it is up to you to do the follow-up and check in with these agencies to learn about the latest audition opportunities.

Of course, everyone says that New York is the place to be if you want to make it big as a fashion model. To a great extent, that is true. Nevertheless, other fashion-driven cities such as Toronto, Los Angeles, Chicago, Dallas, and Atlanta offer a lifetime worth of modeling opportunities, whether they be special events, charity fashion shows, or major advertising campaigns.

Look for ways to get noticed. If you are inclined, participate in beauty pageants or modeling competitions. These are excellent ways to get more exposure, and they look great on a resume.

Specialty Models

Similar to full-body models, specialty models need to present talent agencies with composites of the body part(s) they are modeling. The same kind of scrutiny is necessary in researching agencies and photographers. Because this field is so limited and specialized, however, rarely will you be the victim of a big-time scam.

In fact, most specialty models do this on the side to supplement their incomes from other jobs or to do something unusual. It is important, however, to maintain the beauty of the body parts that will be photographed. If you are a woman and model products that involve only your legs and feet, for example, you must take care to wax your legs and keep your toes from getting blisters.

Teeth—as in toothpaste ads—must be cleaned, polished, and whitened regularly. Hands, which must be consistently manicured, are especially vulnerable to chapping, paper cuts, scratches, and cracked nails. Some models go so far as to have their homes safety proofed. They don't open cans, cut vegetables, or wash dishes. A foot model wouldn't walk long distances, take dance classes, or wear uncomfortable shoes. Someone with perfect teeth wouldn't be caught smoking or eating peanut brittle.

Know that auditions crop up at the oddest hours of the day on very short notice. If you can create a lifestyle that allows you flexible full-time work so that you can readily attend auditions and photo shoots in all parts of the city, then specialty modeling could be an ideal profession for you.

For practice, keep a file of ads that use specialty models. You will find them frequently in food, lifestyle, family, and fashion publications. Then practice various poses in front of a mirror.

Education and Training

How do you develop and perfect your skills?

Runway, Print, and Film Models

No degrees are required for models. However, a savvy knowledge of business transactions is certainly an advantage. And at least some formal training in modeling is also an asset.

Probably the single most crucial requirement is the model's composites, discussed in the previous section. Those, combined with a portfolio of photos and ad tear sheets, give prospective clients a solid idea of how comfortable and creative you can be in front of a camera. A resume listing vital statistics and work experience is also necessary.

Because many runway models also appear in print, they require the same credentials, along with a list of designers and companies for whom they have modeled. It always helps to work with established names, such as Michael Kors, Sue Wong, Thomas Lynch, or Trina Turk. In a business that relies on constant name-dropping, it is a major edge to have worked with such famous personalities.

As we mentioned before, the social scene is the place to be for industry contacts. Hang out at clubs and restaurants that attract a lot of models and designers. Although you must be careful at all times, it is part of models' networking regimens to get their names out to key fashion insiders for career advancement.

Specialty Models

Once again, no formal education is required to succeed as a specialty model. Focus on developing quality composites. Your composites and portfolio are your tickets to being accepted by reliable talent agencies.

Mainly, you need to check in periodically and remind agencies, especially those with high turnover, that you are available for auditions. By always being available for auditions and photo sessions, you will build a reputation for dependability that will get you noticed. The same holds true for showing up early on assignments and being cooperative.

Finally, a good specialty model should feel completely at ease in front of the camera. He or she shouldn't be self-conscious with intense close-ups and must know how to follow specific directions from the photographer and art director. These are skills that come with experience.

Self-Promotion

Here are a few suggestions for effective ways to get your name and face out there.

Runway, Print, and Film Models

Modeling, by nature a show-business-like occupation dependent on hot trends and gorgeous bodies, is driven by prospects who do relentless self-promotion blitzes. When millions of attractive people compete for a limited number of jobs, it goes without saying that certain individuals must get noticed over all the others. That, in a nutshell, is what it takes to make it big—and even to survive.

One of the most frustrating aspects of modeling is that it's a short-lived career. After all, fresh new talent is always on hand to push out the old stalwarts. Accept this fact. Then, work hard to maintain your presence. Change your look. Keep up with the times. Stay in shape. A healthy diet and plenty of exercise should keep you fit for many years.

Once you have appeared on a number of magazine covers, work with your agent to send out news releases about your rising success. Give interviews. Be seen at all kinds of promotions, fundraisers, and society affairs. And be determined to work and travel continuously.

Have your own website and consult reputable modeling websites for trends and job opportunities.

Specialty Models

Vigorous self-promotion is not as crucial to specialty modeling as it is in the general modeling field because your livelihood won't depend totally on this type of work. Yet promotion can help determine how much work you get. You should market yourself to key agencies, as well as keep your composites and portfolios up to date, and even send thank-you notes to the clients with whom you have worked. Primarily, it is important to establish a positive rapport with the talent agencies where you have registered.

Being seen is not so significant here. For the most part, individuals who model certain body parts do not have a desire to be full-time models. They prefer to work in their specialized area, then return to another occupation that fills the bulk of their busy schedules.

Opportunities and Earnings

Salaries vary wildly—not every model is a multimillionaire. Take a look at the range of earnings in this profession.

Runway, Print, and Film Models

One of the most attractive aspects of fashion modeling—besides the glitz and travel opportunities—is the potential to earn an exorbitantly high income. In general, models affiliated with agencies are paid hourly wages for the time it takes to do a photo session. Those rates may be as low as $75 to $150 an hour in smaller markets, or they may range from $200 an hour to $500 or more for top-notch models. A percentage of their earnings goes to the agency that booked them.

Runway models typically get paid a flat fee, ranging from $500 into the thousands for one show. When you enter supermodel terrain, you will find income in the millions. Gisele Bündchen, for example, earned $30 million between June 2005 and June 2006. Her net worth is estimated at $150 million. In addition to traditional modeling duties, some supermodels branch out into other careers. A supermodel may eventually design her own fashions or find work in television or films.

If supermodel stardom is not what you seek, consider working locally. You can earn a comfortable living by modeling locally for catalogs, print ads, runway shows, and special events. Even lesser-known models can earn up to $100,000 per year.

Overall, your exposure will expand since fashion shows and publications have moved to the Internet, where they can be viewed by millions of subscribers. Hence, the modeling profession is far from becoming extinct anytime soon.

Specialty Models

Because specialty modeling is a very small niche market, only a handful of models can make a living from it. You are paid between $175 and $200 an hour for shoots that can take anywhere from two hours to two days. The agency that booked you gets a commission, and you normally wait three months to get paid. You would have to get a lot of assignments to have money on hand to pay the rent.

The select few who have managed to make specialty modeling a career and get steady work can earn annual salaries of $100,000 and beyond. More realistically, this is a part-time profession whose future looks promising as long as there are advertisers who want to showcase their products using certain body parts. Remember that this field's major drawback is its limited access and sporadic employment.

Professional Organizations and Fashion Schools

The organizations and schools listed here can provide further information about opportunities and educational requirements for fashion careers.

American Organizations and Schools

Accrediting Commission of Career Schools and Colleges of
  Technology
2101 Wilson Boulevard, Suite 302
Arlington, VA 22201
www.accsct.org

American Apparel and Footwear Association
1601 North Kent Street, Suite 1200
Arlington, VA 22209
www.apparelandfootwear.org

American Association of University Professors
1012 Fourteenth Street NW, Suite 500
Washington, DC 20005
www.aaup.org

American Federation of Teachers
555 New Jersey Avenue NW
Washington, DC 20001
www.aft.org

American Marketing Association
311 South Wacker Drive, Suite 5800
Chicago, IL 60606
www.ama.org

American Society of Artists
PO Box 1326
Palatine, IL 60078
www.americansocietyofartists.org

American Society of Media Photographers
150 North Second Street
Philadelphia, PA 19106
www.asmp.org

American Society of Photographers
PO Box 1120
Caldwell, TX 77836
www.asofp-online.com

Bulldog Reporter
5900 Hollis Street, Suite L
Emeryville, CA 94608
www.bulldogreporter.com

Cashmere and Camel Hair Manufacturers Institute
6 Beacon Street, Suite 1125
Boston, MA 02108
www.cashmere.org

Career College Association
1101 Connecticut Avenue NW, Suite 900
Washington, DC 20036
www.career.org

Clothing Manufacturers Association of the United States
(CMA)
730 Broadway, Tenth Floor
New York, NY 10003

Clothing and Fashion Industry Model Directory
www.clothingmodel.com

Council of Fashion Designers of America
1412 Broadway, Suite 2006
New York, NY 10018
www.cfda.com

Fashion Group International, Inc.
8 West Fortieth Street, Seventh Floor
New York, NY 10018
www.fgi.org

Fashion Institute of Technology
Seventh Avenue at Twenty-Seventh Street
New York, NY 10001
www.fitnyc.edu

Gemological Institute of America
Robert Mouawad Campus
5345 Armada Drive
Carlsbad, CA 92008
www.gia.edu

Headwear Information Bureau
302 West Twelfth Street, Penthouse C
New York, NY 10014
www.hatsworldwide.com

International Association of Clothing Designers and
    Executives
835 Northwest Thirty-Sixth Terrace
Oklahoma City, OK 73118
www.iacde.com

International Formalwear Association
401 North Michigan Avenue
Chicago, IL 60611
www.formalwear.org

International Mass Retail Association
1700 North Moore Street, Suite 2250
Arlington, VA 22209

International Modeling and Talent Association
www.imta.com

International Swimwear/Activewear Market
13351-D Riverside Drive, Suite 658
Sherman Oaks, CA 91423
www.isamla.com

Jewelers of America
52 Vanderbilt Avenue, Nineteenth Floor
New York, NY 10017
www.jewelers.org

Magazine Publishers of America
810 Seventh Avenue, Twenty-Fourth Floor
New York, NY 10019
www.magazine.org

Manufacturers' Agents National Association
One Spectrum Pointe, Suite 150
Lake Forest, CA 92630
www.manaonline.org

Manufacturing Jewelers and Suppliers of America
45 Royal Little Drive
Providence, RI 02904
www.mjsa.org

National Art Education Association
1916 Association Drive
Reston, VA 20191
www.naea-reston.org

National Association of Schools of Art and Design
11250 Roger Bacon Drive, Suite 21
Reston, VA 20190
www.arts-accredit.org

National Fashion Accessories Association
350 Fifth Avenue, Suite 2030
New York, NY 10118
www.accessoryweb.com

National Outerwear and Sportswear Association
240 Madison Avenue, Twelfth Floor
New York, NY 10016

National Press Photographers Association
3200 Croasdaile Drive, Suite 306
Durham, NC 27705
www.nppa.org

National Textile Association
6 Beacon Street, Suite 1125
Boston, MA 02108
www.nationaltextile.org

Neckwear Association of America
151 Lexington Avenue, Suite 2-F
New York, NY 10016

The Newspaper Guild
501 Third Street NW
Washington, DC 20001
www.newsguild.org

Parsons The New School for Design
66 Fifth Avenue, Suite 6
New York, NY 10011
www.parsons.edu

Professional Photographers of America
229 Peachtree Street NE, Suite 2200
Atlanta, GA 30303
www.ppa.com

Public Relations Society of America
33 Maiden Lane, Eleventh Floor
New York, NY 10038
www.prsa.org

Retail Merchants Association
5101 Monument Avenue
Richmond, VA 23230
www.retailmerchants.com

Shoe Service Institute of America
18 School Street
North Brookfield, MA 01535
www.ssia.info

UNITE HERE
(formerly the Union of Needletrades, Industrial, and Textile
    Employees and the Hotel Employees and Restaurant
    Employees International Union)
275 Seventh Avenue
New York, NY 10001
www.unitehere.org

Canadian Organizations and Schools

Academy of Fashion Design
218-B Avenue B South
Saskatoon, SK S7M 1M4
Canada
www.aofdesign.com

Alberta College of Art and Design
1407-14 Avenue NW
Calgary, AB T2N 4R3
Canada
www.acad.ab.ca

Apparel and Textile Association of Saskatchewan
1102 H Avenue
Saskatoon, SK S4P 3C2
Canada

Apparel BC
1859 Franklin Street
Vancouver, BC V5L 1P9
Canada
www.apparel-bc.org

Art Institute of Vancouver
700-1090 West Georgia Street
Vancouver, BC V6E 3V7
Canada
www.wherecreativitygoestoschool.ca

Association of Clothing Manufacturing of the Province of
   Quebec
801-555 Chabanel West, Suite 801
Montreal, QC H2N 2H8
Canada

Association of Sewn Alberta Products
319 Queen Charlotte Place SE
Calgary, AB T2J 4H8
Canada
www.albertasews.com

Canadian Apparel Federation
124 O'Connor Street, Suite 504
Ottawa, ON K1P 5M9
Canada
www.apparel.ca

Canadian Association of Wholesale Sales Representatives
1771 Avenue Road
PO Box 54546
Toronto, ON M5M 4N5
Canada
www.caws.ca

Canadian Textiles Institute
222 Somerset Street West, Suite 500
Ottawa, ON K2P 2G3
Canada
www.textiles.ca

Children's Apparel Manufacturers Association
6900 Decarie Boulevard, Suite 3110
Montreal, QC H3X 2T8
Canada

College of the North Atlantic—Textile Studies
Bay St. George Campus
PO Box 5400
Stephenville, NL A2N 2Z6
Canada
www.cna.nl.ca

Design Exchange
234 Bay Street
PO Box 18
Toronto Dominion Center
Toronto, ON M5K 1B2
Canada
www.dx.org

Fashion Design Council of Canada
55 Avenue Road, Suite 2350
Toronto, ON M5R 3L2
Canada
www.lorealfashionweek.ca

Fur Council of Canada
1435 St. Alexandre, Suite 1270
Montreal, QC H3A 2G4
Canada
www.furcouncil.com

Furriers Guild of Canada
211-4174 Dundas Street West
Toronto, ON M8X 1X3
Canada

George Brown College
Centre for Fashions Studies and Jewellery
Casa Loma Campus
160 Kendal Avenue
Toronto, ON M5R 1M3
Canada
www.georgebrown.ca

International Academy of Design and Technology
39 John Street
Toronto, ON M5V 3G6
Canada
www.iadt.ca

Manitoba Fashion Institute
165 Selkirk Avenue East, Third Floor
Winnipeg, MB R2W 2L3
Canada
www.apparel-manitoba.org

Men's Clothing Manufacturing Association
801-555 Chabanel West
Montreal, QC H2N 2H8
Canada

New Brunswick College of Craft and Design
457 Queen Street
PO Box 6000
Fredericton, NB E3B 5H1
Canada
www.nbccd.ca

Ontario Fabricare Association
55A Woodbury Road
Toronto, ON M8W 1X8
Canada
www.fabricare.org

Ontario Fashion Exhibitors
160 Tycos Drive, Suite 2219
Box 218
Toronto, ON M6B 1W8
Canada
www.ontariofashionexhibitors.ca

Shoe Manufacturers Association of Canada
PO Box 223
Beaconsfield, QC H9W 5T7
Canada
www.shoecanada.com

Toronto Fashion Incubator
285 Manitoba Drive
Exhibition Place
Toronto, ON M6K 3C3
Canada
www.fashionincubator.com

UNITE HERE Canada
460 Richmond Street West, Second Floor
Toronto, ON M5V 1Y1
Canada
www.unitehere.ca

For Further Reading

R efer to the following publications and resources for more information about careers in the world of fashion.

Career Resources

Occupational Outlook Handbook. Washington, DC: Bureau of Labor Statistics, Superintendent of Documents, U.S. Government Printing Office, Updated biannually. Available online at www.bls.gov/oco.

Encyclopedia of Careers and Vocational Guidance, 14th ed. New York: Ferguson Publishing Company, 2007.

Books

Antongiavanni, Nicholas. *The Suit: A Machiavellian Approach to Men's Style.* New York: HarperCollins, 2006.

Blackman, Cally. *100 Years of Fashion Illustration.* London: Laurence King Publishing, Ltd., 2007.

Brown, Bobbi. *Bobbi Brown Living Beauty.* New York: Springboard Press, 2007.

Buxbaum, Gerda. *Icons of Fashion: The 20th Century*, 2nd ed. New York: Prestel Publishing, 2005.

Dawber, Martin. *Big Book of Fashion Illustration: A World Sourcebook of Contemporary Illustration*. London: B.T. Batsford Ltd., 2007.

Gehlhar, Mary. *The Fashion Designer Survival Guide: An Insider's Look at Starting and Running Your Own Fashion Business*. New York: Kaplan Business, 2005.

Gunn, Tim, and Kate Moloney. *Tim Gunn: A Guide to Quality, Taste and Style*. New York: Abrams Image, 2007.

Helleu, Jacques, and Laurence Benaim. *Jacques Helleu and Chanel*. New York: Harry N. Abrams, 2006.

Karapetyan, Berta. *Runway Knits: 30 Fashion-Forward Designs*. New York: Potter Craft, 2007.

McDowell, Colin. *Ralph Lauren: The Man, the Vision, the Style*. New York: Rizzoli, 2003.

Nicolay, Megan. *Generation T: 108 Ways to Transform a T-Shirt*. New York: Workman Publishing Company, 2006.

Oliva, Alberto, and Norberto Angeletti. *In Vogue: The Illustrated History of the World's Most Famous Fashion Magazine*. New York: Rizzoli, 2006.

Porizkova, Paulina. *A Model Summer: A Novel*. New York: Hyperion, 2007.

Rannels, Melissa, Melissa Alvarado, and Hope Meng. *Sew Subversive: Down and Dirty DIY for the Fabulous Fashionista*. Newtown, CT: Taunton Press, 2006.

Steele, Valerie. *Shoes: A Lexicon of Style*. London: Scriptum Editions, 2006.

Tatham, Caroline. *Fashion Design Drawing Course*. Hauppauge, NY: Barron's Educational Series, 2003.

Waddell, Gavin. *How Fashion Works: Couture, Ready-to-Wear and Mass Production*. Oxford: Blackwell Publishing, Ltd., 2004.

Wilcox, Claire, and Vivienne Westwood. *Vivienne Westwood*. New York: Harry N. Abrams, 2005.

About the Author

··

Chicago writer Lucia Mauro penned VGM's *Career Portraits: Fashion* and has written about fashion and design for a variety of publications, such as *Chicago Social* and *Windy City Woman*. She writes frequently about the performing arts for the *Chicago Tribune, Chicago Magazine, The Chicago Collection,* and national arts magazines, including *Dance Magazine, Dance Teacher, Pointe Magazine,* and *Stage Directions.* Mauro is the author of McGraw-Hill's *Careers for the Stagestruck & Other Dramatic Types* (now in its second edition), and she is a regular arts contributor to Chicago Public Radio and a national public speaker on arts-related subjects.

Mauro, who frequently travels to Italy, is also an accomplished photographer and has published two books of her architectural photography: *Frieze Frame: Textures & Colors of Italy* (2004) and *Frieze Frame II: Textures & Colors of Italy* (2006). She exhibits her work in galleries and cultural institutions. For more information, visit www.luciamauro.com.